Building RESTful API
with DynamoDB
and PostgreSQL

With its clear explanations, captivating examples, and practical
exercises, you'll be crafting state-of-the-art APIs in no time.

Katie Millie

Building RESTful API with DynamoDB and PostgreSQL

With its clear explanations, captivating examples, and practical exercises, you'll be crafting state-of-the-art APIs in no time.

By

Katie Millie

Copyright notice

Copyright © 2024 Katie Millie. All rights reserved.

Unauthorized reproduction, distribution, or transmission of any part of this content through any medium—such as photocopying, recording, or via electronic or mechanical means—is strictly prohibited without the explicit written permission of the author. This prohibition extends to all forms of content sharing except for brief quotations used in critical reviews or other specific noncommercial purposes that are legally permitted by copyright law. Any violation of these terms will result in legal consequences.

Table of contents

INTRODUCTION

Chapter 1

    The Rise of Connected Applications: Why APIs Matter Now More Than Ever

        Demystifying APIs: The Language of Communication Between ApplicationsIn the modern era of technology

            Choosing the Right Database: A Balancing Act for Modern APIs

Chapter 2

    Unveiling REST: Building User-Friendly APIs

        Designing RESTful Endpoints: Crafting Clear and Consistent API Interactions

            Building a Strong Foundation: Tools and Technologies for Building RESTful APIs

Chapter 3

    Introduction to DynamoDB: A NoSQL Database Built for High Performance

        Data Modeling with DynamoDB: Understanding Tables, Primary Keys, and Attributes

            Performing CRUD Operations with DynamoDB: Creating, Reading, Updating, and Deleting Data Effectively

                Scaling with Confidence: DynamoDB's Auto-Scaling and Partitioning Strategies

Chapter 4

    Introduction to PostgreSQL: A Relational Database for Structured Data Management

Creating Powerful Schemas: Defining Tables, Entities, and Relationships in PostgreSQL

Performing SQL Operations with Confidence: Crafting Queries for Data Retrieval and Manipulation

Ensuring Data Integrity: Constraints, Transactions, and Maintaining Data Consistency in PostgreSQL

Chapter 5

Understanding the Integration Landscape: Choosing the Right Approach for Your Needs

Utilizing Event-Driven Architecture: Leveraging Triggers and Streams for Real-Time Data Synchronization

Building a Hybrid Data Model: Mapping Data Between DynamoDB and PostgreSQL Effectively

Best Practices for Integration: Optimizing Performance, Reliability, and Scalability

Chapter 6

Designing the Data Model: Separating User Profiles (PostgreSQL) and Real-Time Activity (DynamoDB)

Building Endpoints for User Management: User Registration, Login, and Profile Management (PostgreSQL)

Implementing Real-Time Features: Notifications and Updates powered by DynamoDB

Securing Your Social Media Platform: Authentication and Authorization Strategies

Building a High-Traffic E-Commerce

Platform: Balancing Product Catalog (PostgreSQL) with Shopping Cart and Order Processing (DynamoDB)

Chapter 7

Building a Real-Time IoT Application: Collecting sensor data from devices (DynamoDB) and analyzing trends (PostgreSQL)

Building a Scalable Content Management System: User-Generated Content and Media Files (DynamoDB) with Post Metadata (PostgreSQL)

Chapter 8

Authentication and Authorization: Implementing User Access Control Mechanisms in a RESTful API with DynamoDB and PostgreSQL

Data Validation and Sanitization: Preventing Malicious Data Injection Attacks in a RESTful API with DynamoDB and PostgreSQL

Securing Communication Channels: Utilizing Encryption for Secure Data Transfer

Monitoring and Logging: Keeping Track of API Activity and Identifying Potential Issues

Chapter 9

Choosing the Right Deployment Environment: Cloud or On-Premises Considerations

Configuration for Deployment: Optimizing Your API for Production Usage

Monitoring and Maintaining Your API: Keeping Your Creation Running Smoothly

Conclusion

Appendix

Glossary of Terms
  Common Libraries and Frameworks for Building APIs with DynamoDB and PostgreSQL

INTRODUCTION

Building RESTful API with DynamoDB and PostgreSQL: The Power Couple of Modern Data

Do you dream of building the next big app, a seamless integration between services, or a website that communicates with lightning speed? The secret weapon lies in **RESTful APIs** (Application Programming Interfaces). But venturing into this exciting world can feel like navigating a maze – where do you even begin, and which database to choose? Fear not, fellow developer! "Building RESTful API with DynamoDB and PostgreSQL" is your ultimate guide, unlocking the power of this dynamic duo for crafting robust and scalable APIs.

This book isn't your typical technical tome. We'll ditch the sleep-inducing jargon and embark on a thrilling journey, equipping you with the knowledge to build APIs that sing. Imagine yourself as a data architect, wielding the combined might of DynamoDB, the blazing-fast NoSQL hero, and PostgreSQL, the relational database champion. Together, they'll form the foundation for your API masterpiece!

But why this specific combination? Here's the magic:

- **DynamoDB**: For data that needs high scalability and blazing-fast reads and writes, DynamoDB is your knight in shining armor. It's perfect for

handling massive datasets, user accounts, or real-time data streams.
- **PostgreSQL**: When you need the power of structured data and complex queries, PostgreSQL steps in. This relational database powerhouse excels in managing intricate relationships between data points, ideal for product catalogs, user profiles, or order history.

By harnessing the strengths of both, you'll build an API capable of handling the most demanding workloads. This book will equip you with the knowledge to:

- **Master the Art of RESTful APIs**: We'll demystify RESTful architecture, teaching you how to design clear, consistent, and user-friendly APIs.
- **Embrace the Power of DynamoDB**: Learn how to model data in DynamoDB, perform efficient CRUD (Create, Read, Update, Delete) operations, and leverage its scalability for massive datasets.
- **Unleash the Relational Power of PostgreSQL**: Dive deep into PostgreSQL's world, creating tables with rich relationships, crafting powerful queries, and ensuring data integrity.
- **Connect the Titans**: Learn how to integrate DynamoDB and PostgreSQL seamlessly, leveraging their strengths for a truly robust data management solution.
- **Build Real-World APIs**: Put your newfound knowledge into action! We'll explore use cases like building a social media platform with user

profiles in PostgreSQL and real-time notifications powered by DynamoDB.
- **Secure Your Creation**: Learn essential security practices to protect your API from unauthorized access and data breaches.

"**Building RESTful API with DynamoDB and PostgreSQL**" is more than just a book; it's your launchpad into the exciting world of API development. With its clear explanations, captivating examples, and practical exercises, you'll be crafting state-of-the-art APIs in no time. So, grab your coding tools, and let's embark on this thrilling adventure together! We'll build APIs that are not just functional, but truly impressive and powerful.

Chapter 1

The Rise of Connected Applications: Why APIs Matter Now More Than Ever

In today's digital era, the concept of connected applications is not just a trend but a necessity. As businesses and developers seek to create more integrated and interactive experiences, APIs (Application Programming Interfaces) have emerged as the backbone of modern software development. APIs enable disparate systems to communicate and share data seamlessly, making them crucial for building robust, scalable, and efficient applications. This article delves into why APIs matter now more than ever, with a focus on building RESTful APIs using DynamoDB and PostgreSQL.

Understanding APIs and Their Importance

APIs are sets of rules and protocols that allow different software entities to interact with each other. They define the methods and data formats that applications use to communicate, ensuring interoperability and data exchange. Here are several reasons why APIs are vital in the contemporary digital landscape:

1. Integration: APIs allow for the integration of services and data across various platforms and applications. This capability is essential for creating seamless user experiences.

2. Scalability: By leveraging APIs, developers can build scalable applications that can handle growing amounts of traffic and data.

3. Innovation: APIs facilitate rapid development and innovation by allowing developers to utilize existing services and tools rather than building from scratch.

4. Flexibility: They provide flexibility to developers to choose the best tools and technologies for different parts of an application.

5. Efficiency: APIs streamline development processes and reduce time-to-market by enabling the reuse of existing components and services.

Building RESTful APIs with DynamoDB and PostgreSQL

REST (Representational State Transfer) is an architectural style for designing networked applications. It uses standard HTTP methods and status codes, making it straightforward and easy to implement. Here, we will explore building RESTful APIs using two popular databases: DynamoDB and PostgreSQL.

DynamoDB

Amazon DynamoDB is a fully managed NoSQL database service that provides fast and predictable performance with seamless scalability. It's ideal for applications that require high throughput and low latency at any scale.

Setting Up DynamoDB

First, we need to set up DynamoDB and create a table. In this example, we'll create a table for storing user data.

```python
import boto3

# Initialize a session using Amazon DynamoDB
dynamodb = boto3.resource('dynamodb', region_name='us-west-2')

# Create the DynamoDB table
table = dynamodb.create_table(
    TableName='Users',
    KeySchema=[
        {
            'AttributeName': 'user_id',
            'KeyType': 'HASH'  # Partition key
```

```
        }
    AttributeDefinitions=[
        {
            'AttributeName': 'user_id',
            'AttributeType': 'S'
        }
    ProvisionedThroughput={
        'ReadCapacityUnits': 5,
        'WriteCapacityUnits': 5
}

# Wait until the table exists.
table.meta.client.get_waiter('table_exists').wait(TableName='Users')

print("Table status:", table.table_status)
```

Building a RESTful API with DynamoDB

Next, we'll create a simple RESTful API using Flask, a popular Python web framework. This API will perform basic CRUD (Create, Read, Update, Delete) operations on the DynamoDB table.

```python
from flask import Flask, request, jsonify
import boto3
```

```python
from boto3.dynamodb.conditions import Key

app = Flask(__name__)
dynamodb = boto3.resource('dynamodb', region_name='us-west-2')
table = dynamodb.Table('Users')

@app.route('/users', methods=['POST'])
def create_user():
    user_id = request.json['user_id']
    name = request.json['name']
    email = request.json['email']

    table.put_item(
        Item={
            'user_id': user_id,
            'name': name,
            'email': cmail
        }
    )

    return jsonify({'message': 'User created successfully'}), 201

@app.route('/users/<user_id>', methods=['GET'])
def get_user(user_id):
    response = table.get_item(
        Key={
            'user_id': user_id
```

```python
        }

    if 'Item' in response:
        return jsonify(response['Item'])
    else:
        return jsonify({'message': 'User not found'}), 404

@app.route('/users/<user_id>', methods=['PUT'])
def update_user(user_id):
    name = request.json['name']
    email = request.json['email']

    table.update_item(
        Key={
            'user_id': user_id
        },
        UpdateExpression="set #n=:n, email=:e",
        ExpressionAttributeValues={
            ':n': name,
            ':e': email
        },
        ExpressionAttributeNames={
            "#n": "name"
        }
    )

    return jsonify({'message': 'User updated successfully'})
```

```
@app.route('/users/<user_id>', methods=['DELETE'])
def delete_user(user_id):
    table.delete_item(
        Key={
            'user_id': user_id
        }
    )
    return jsonify({'message': 'User deleted successfully'})

if __name__ == '__main__':
    app.run(debug=True)
```

PostgreSQL

PostgreSQL is a powerful, open-source relational database system with a strong reputation for reliability, feature robustness, and performance.

Setting Up PostgreSQL

First, install PostgreSQL and create a database. Once installed, use the `psql` command-line tool to create a database and a table.

```sql
CREATE DATABASE userdb;
\c userdb
```

```sql
CREATE TABLE users (
    user_id SERIAL PRIMARY KEY,
    name VARCHAR(100),
    email VARCHAR(100)
);
```

Building a RESTful API with PostgreSQL

We'll use Flask along with `psycopg2`, a PostgreSQL adapter for Python, to build a RESTful API.

```python
from flask import Flask, request, jsonify
import psycopg2

app = Flask(__name__)

conn = psycopg2.connect(
    database="userdb",
    user="yourusername",
    password="yourpassword",
    host="127.0.0.1",
    port="5432"
)
cursor = conn.cursor()
```

```python
@app.route('/users', methods=['POST'])
def create_user():
    name = request.json['name']
    email = request.json['email']

    cursor.execute("INSERT INTO users (name, email) VALUES (%s, %s) RETURNING user_id", (name, email))
    user_id = cursor.fetchone()[0]
    conn.commit()

    return jsonify({'user_id': user_id, 'message': 'User created successfully'}), 201

@app.route('/users/<int:user_id>', methods=['GET'])
def get_user(user_id):
    cursor.execute("SELECT * FROM users WHERE user_id = %s", (user_id,))
    user = cursor.fetchone()

    if user:
        return jsonify({'user_id': user[0], 'name': user[1], 'email': user[2]})
    else:
        return jsonify({'message': 'User not found'}), 404

@app.route('/users/<int:user_id>', methods=['PUT'])
def update_user(user_id):
```

```python
        name = request.json['name']
        email = request.json['email']

        cursor.execute("UPDATE users SET name = %s, email = %s WHERE user_id = %s", (name, email, user_id))
        conn.commit()

        return jsonify({'message': 'User updated successfully'})

    @app.route('/users/<int:user_id>', methods=['DELETE'])
    def delete_user(user_id):
        cursor.execute("DELETE FROM users WHERE user_id = %s", (user_id,))
        conn.commit()

        return jsonify({'message': 'User deleted successfully'})

    if __name__ == '__main__':
        app.run(debug=True)
```
```

## **Why APIs Matter More Than Ever**
```

In the age of digital transformation, the role of APIs has become more critical than ever. Here are some reasons why:

1. Ecosystem Building: APIs enable companies to create ecosystems by allowing third-party developers to build on their platforms. This approach not only enhances the functionality of their services but also drives innovation and user engagement.

2. Data-Driven Decisions: APIs facilitate the integration of analytics and data collection tools, empowering organizations to make data-driven decisions.

3. Agility and Speed: APIs enable agile development methodologies, allowing teams to iterate quickly and release features faster.

4. Cross-Platform Compatibility: With the rise of mobile and web applications, APIs ensure that services are accessible across different platforms, providing a consistent user experience.

5. Monetization Opportunities: Many organizations have leveraged APIs to create new revenue streams by offering their services and data to external developers and businesses.

APIs are the cornerstone of modern application development. They enable integration, scalability, and innovation, making them indispensable in today's connected world. Whether using NoSQL databases like DynamoDB or relational databases like PostgreSQL, building RESTful APIs allows developers to create powerful and efficient applications. As businesses continue to embrace digital transformation, the importance of APIs will only grow, driving the future of connected applications.

Demystifying APIs: The Language of Communication Between ApplicationsIn the modern era of technology

APIs (Application Programming Interfaces) serve as the cornerstone for enabling seamless communication between different software applications. They allow disparate systems to interact and share data, fostering a more integrated and efficient digital ecosystem. Understanding how APIs work and how to build them is essential for developers looking to create scalable and robust applications. This article demystifies APIs and explores building RESTful APIs using two popular databases: DynamoDB and PostgreSQL.

What Are APIs?

APIs are sets of rules and protocols that allow one software application to interact with another. They define the methods and data structures that developers can use to communicate with various services. APIs can be classified into several types, including REST (Representational State Transfer), SOAP (Simple Object Access Protocol), and GraphQL, with REST being the most commonly used architectural style in modern web development.

Why Are APIs Important?

APIs play a crucial role in today's digital landscape for several reasons:

1. Interoperability: APIs enable different systems to work together, allowing for the integration of services across various platforms.

2. Scalable: By decoupling different components of an application, APIs facilitate scaling individual parts without affecting the whole system.

3. Innovation: APIs provide developers with the flexibility to use existing services and build upon them, fostering innovation and reducing development time.

4. Efficiency: Reusing existing APIs saves time and resources, allowing developers to focus on building unique features.

5. User Experience: APIs enable seamless data sharing and integration, leading to enhanced user experiences.

Building RESTful APIs with DynamoDB and PostgreSQL

RESTful APIs adhere to REST principles, using standard HTTP methods such as GET, POST, PUT, and DELETE. Here, we'll explore how to build RESTful APIs using DynamoDB, a NoSQL database, and PostgreSQL, a relational database.

Setting Up DynamoDB

Amazon DynamoDB is a fully managed NoSQL database service known for its high performance and scalability. To get started with DynamoDB, we need to set up the database and create a table.

Creating a DynamoDB Table

First, we'll use the AWS SDK for Python, Boto3, to create a DynamoDB table for storing user data.

```python
import boto3

# Initialize a session using Amazon DynamoDB
dynamodb = boto3.resource('dynamodb', region_name='us-west-2')

# Create the DynamoDB table
table = dynamodb.create_table(
    TableName='Users',
    KeySchema=[
        {
            'AttributeName': 'user_id',
            'KeyType': 'HASH'  # Partition key
        }
    AttributeDefinitions=[
        {
            'AttributcNamc': 'user_id',
            'AttributeType': 'S'
        }
    ProvisionedThroughput={
        'ReadCapacityUnits': 5,
        'WriteCapacityUnits': 5
    }

# Wait until the table exists.
table.meta.client.get_waiter('table_exists').wait(TableName='Users')
```

```
print("Table status:", table.table_status)
```

Building a RESTful API with DynamoDB

Next, we'll create a simple RESTful API using Flask, a Python web framework, to perform CRUD operations on the DynamoDB table.

```python
from flask import Flask, request, jsonify
import boto3
from boto3.dynamodb.conditions import Key

app = Flask(__name__)
dynamodb = boto3.resource('dynamodb', region_name='us-west-2')
table = dynamodb.Table('Users')

@app.route('/users', methods=['POST'])
def create_user():
    user_id = request.json['user_id']
    name = request.json['name']
    email = request.json['email']

    table.put_item(
        Item={
```

```
        'user_id': user_id,
        'name': name,
        'email': email
    }
    return jsonify({'message': 'User created successfully'}), 201

@app.route('/users/<user_id>', methods=['GET'])
def get_user(user_id):
    response = table.get_item(
        Key={
            'user_id': user_id
        }
    )
    if 'Item' in response:
        return jsonify(response['Item'])
    else:
        return jsonify({'message': 'User not found'}), 404

@app.route('/users/<user_id>', methods=['PUT'])
def update_user(user_id):
    name = request.json['name']
    email = request.json['email']

    table.update_item(
        Key={
            'user_id': user_id
        },
        UpdateExpression="set #n=:n, email=:e",
```

```
        ExpressionAttributeValues={
           ':n': name,
           ':e': email
        },
        ExpressionAttributeNames={
           "#n": "name"
        }

    return jsonify({'message': 'User updated successfully'})

@app.route('/users/<user_id>', methods=['DELETE'])
def delete_user(user_id):
    table.delete_item(
       Key={
          'user_id': user_id
       }
    )

    return jsonify({'message': 'User deleted successfully'})

if __name__ == '__main__':
    app.run(debug=True)
```

Setting Up PostgreSQL

PostgreSQL is a powerful, open-source relational database system. To use PostgreSQL, we first need to set up the database and create a table.

Creating a PostgreSQL Database and Table

We'll use the `psql` command-line tool to create a database and a table.

```sql
CREATE DATABASE userdb;
\c userdb

CREATE TABLE users (
    user_id SERIAL PRIMARY KEY,
    name VARCHAR(100),
    email VARCHAR(100)
);
```

Building a RESTful API with PostgreSQL

We'll use Flask along with `psycopg2`, a PostgreSQL adapter for Python, to build a RESTful API.

```python
from flask import Flask, request, jsonify
import psycopg2
```

```python
app = Flask(__name__)

conn = psycopg2.connect(
    database="userdb",
    user="yourusername",
    password="yourpassword",
    host="127.0.0.1",
    port="5432"
)
cursor = conn.cursor()

@app.route('/users', methods=['POST'])
def create_user():
    name = request.json['name']
    email = request.json['email']

    cursor.execute("INSERT INTO users (name, email) VALUES (%s, %s) RETURNING user_id", (name, email))
    user_id = cursor.fetchone()[0]
    conn.commit()

    return jsonify({'user_id': user_id, 'message': 'User created successfully'}), 201

@app.route('/users/<int:user_id>', methods=['GET'])
def get_user(user_id):
```

```python
    cursor.execute("SELECT * FROM users WHERE user_id = %s", (user_id,))
    user = cursor.fetchone()

    if user:
        return jsonify({'user_id': user[0], 'name': user[1], 'email': user[2]})
    else:
        return jsonify({'message': 'User not found'}), 404

@app.route('/users/<int:user_id>', methods=['PUT'])
def update_user(user_id):
    name = request.json['name']
    email = request.json['email']

    cursor.execute("UPDATE users SET name = %s, email = %s WHERE user_id = %s", (name, email, user_id))
    conn.commit()

    return jsonify({'message': 'User updated successfully'})

@app.route('/users/<int:user_id>', methods=['DELETE'])
def delete_user(user_id):
    cursor.execute("DELETE FROM users WHERE user_id = %s", (user_id,))
```

```
        conn.commit()

        return jsonify({'message': 'User deleted successfully'})

if __name__ == '__main__':
    app.run(debug=True)
```

Bridging the Two Worlds

While both DynamoDB and PostgreSQL serve as databases, they cater to different use cases. DynamoDB's NoSQL architecture is perfect for applications requiring high throughput and low latency, making it ideal for real-time data processing. PostgreSQL, with its robust SQL capabilities, is excellent for applications requiring complex queries and transactions.

APIs bridge the gap between these different database architectures, enabling applications to leverage the strengths of both. For instance, an e-commerce application might use DynamoDB to handle high-velocity transactional data and PostgreSQL for analytical and reporting purposes.

The Language of APIs

APIs, particularly RESTful ones, communicate using standard HTTP methods:

- **GET**: Retrieve data from a server.

- **POST**: Send data to the server to create a new resource.

- **PUT**: Update an existing resource on the server.

- **DELETE**: Remove a resource from the server.

These methods correspond to the CRUD operations (Create, Read, Update, Delete), making it easy for developers to understand and implement.

APIs are the language of communication between applications, enabling interoperability, scalability, and innovation. Understanding how to build RESTful APIs using databases like DynamoDB and PostgreSQL is crucial for modern software development. By leveraging the strengths of both NoSQL and SQL databases, developers can create powerful, efficient, and scalable applications that meet the diverse needs of today's digital landscape.

Demystifying APIs and mastering their implementation is a significant step towards building robust and connected applications. As the digital world continues to evolve, the role of APIs will only become more central, driving the future of software development and integration.

Choosing the Right Database: A Balancing Act for Modern APIs

In the realm of modern software development, the database you choose for your application can profoundly impact its performance, scalability, and maintainability. With the rise of APIs (Application Programming Interfaces) as the standard for communication between software components, selecting the right database is crucial. This article explores the nuances of choosing between two popular databases, DynamoDB and PostgreSQL, and provides examples of building RESTful APIs with each.

The Importance of Database Selection

When designing an API, the choice of database affects:

1. Performance: Different databases offer varied read/write speeds and handling capabilities for large datasets

2. Scalability: As your application grows, the database must be able to scale horizontally or vertically.

3. Consistency and Availability: Balancing the CAP theorem (Consistency, Availability, and Partition Tolerance) is crucial for ensuring data integrity and accessibility.

4. Flexibility: Some databases offer more flexibility in terms of schema design and data modeling.

5. Complexity of Queries: The type of queries your application requires will influence whether a NoSQL or SQL database is more suitable.

DynamoDB vs. PostgreSQL

DynamoDB

DynamoDB is a fully managed NoSQL database service provided by Amazon Web Services (AWS). It is known for its high performance, scalability, and ability to handle large amounts of traffic with low latency.

Pros:

- **Scalability**: Automatically scales to handle large amounts of data and high traffic.

- **Performance**: Optimized for fast read/write operations.

- **Fully Managed:** AWS handles maintenance, backups, and security.

Cons:

- **Complex Queries:** Limited support for complex queries and transactions compared to SQL databases.

- **Cost**: Pricing can become expensive with high read/write operations.

PostgreSQL

PostgreSQL is an open-source relational database system renowned for its robustness, feature set, and performance.

Pros:

- **Complex Queries:** Excellent support for complex queries, joins, and transactions.

- **ACID Compliance:** Ensures data consistency and integrity.

- **Extensibility**: Supports custom functions and data types.

Cons:

- **Scalability**: Scaling can be more challenging and may require more manual intervention compared to NoSQL databases.

- **Performance**: Might not match the low-latency performance of NoSQL databases for certain use cases.

Building RESTful APIs with DynamoDB

To demonstrate the capabilities of DynamoDB, let's build a simple RESTful API for managing user data using Flask and Boto3, AWS's SDK for Python.

Setting Up DynamoDB

First, we need to set up DynamoDB and create a table for users.

```python
```

```python
import boto3

# Initialize a session using Amazon DynamoDB
dynamodb = boto3.resource('dynamodb', region_name='us-west-2')

# Create the DynamoDB table
table = dynamodb.create_table(
    TableName='Users',
    KeySchema=[
        {
            'AttributeName': 'user_id',
            'KeyType': 'HASH'  # Partition key
        }
    AttributeDefinitions=[
        {
            'AttributeName': 'user_id',
            'AttributeType': 'S'
        }
    ProvisionedThroughput={
        'ReadCapacityUnits': 5,
        'WriteCapacityUnits': 5
    }

# Wait until the table exists.
table.meta.client.get_waiter('table_exists').wait(TableName='Users')
```

```
print("Table status:", table.table_status)
```

Building the API

Next, we create a Flask application to perform CRUD operations on the DynamoDB table.

```python
from flask import Flask, request, jsonify
import boto3
from boto3.dynamodb.conditions import Key

app = Flask(__name__)
dynamodb = boto3.resource('dynamodb', region_name='us-west-2')
table = dynamodb.Table('Users')

@app.route('/users', methods=['POST'])
def create_user():
    user_id = request.json['user_id']
    name = request.json['name']
    email = request.json['email']

    table.put_item(
      Item={
        'user_id': user_id,
        'name': name,
```

```python
        'email': email
    }

    return jsonify({'message': 'User created successfully'}), 201

@app.route('/users/<user_id>', methods=['GET'])
def get_user(user_id):
    response = table.get_item(
        Key={
            'user_id': user_id
        }
    )

    if 'Item' in response:
        return jsonify(response['Item'])
    else:
        return jsonify({'message': 'User not found'}), 404

@app.route('/users/<user_id>', methods=['PUT'])
def update_user(user_id):
    name = request.json['name']
    email = request.json['email']

    table.update_item(
        Key={
            'user_id': user_id
        },
        UpdateExpression="set #n=:n, email=:e",
```

```
    ExpressionAttributeValues={
      ':n': name,
      ':e': email
    },
    ExpressionAttributeNames={
      "#n": "name"
    }

  return jsonify({'message': 'User updated successfully'})

@app.route('/users/<user_id>', methods=['DELETE'])
def delete_user(user_id):
  table.delete_item(
    Key={
      'user_id': user_id
    }

  return jsonify({'message': 'User deleted successfully'})

if __name__ == '__main__':
  app.run(debug=True)
```
```

## Building RESTful APIs with PostgreSQL

Now, let's build a similar RESTful API using PostgreSQL. PostgreSQL excels at handling complex
```

queries and transactions, making it a great choice for relational data.

Setting Up PostgreSQL

We start by installing PostgreSQL and creating a database and table for users.

```sql
CREATE DATABASE userdb;
\c userdb

CREATE TABLE users (
    user_id SERIAL PRIMARY KEY,
    name VARCHAR(100),
    email VARCHAR(100)
);
```

Building the API

We use Flask along with `psycopg2`, a PostgreSQL adapter for Python, to create the RESTful API.

```python
from flask import Flask, request, jsonify
import psycopg2
```

```python
app = Flask(__name__)

conn = psycopg2.connect(
    database="userdb",
    user="yourusername",
    password="yourpassword",
    host="127.0.0.1",
    port="5432"
)
cursor = conn.cursor()

@app.route('/users', methods=['POST'])
def create_user():
    name = request.json['name']
    email = request.json['email']

    cursor.execute("INSERT INTO users (name, email) VALUES (%s, %s) RETURNING user_id", (name, email))
    user_id = cursor.fetchone()[0]
    conn.commit()

    return jsonify({'user_id': user_id, 'message': 'User created successfully'}), 201

@app.route('/users/<int:user_id>', methods=['GET'])
def get_user(user_id):
```

```python
    cursor.execute("SELECT * FROM users WHERE user_id = %s", (user_id,))
    user = cursor.fetchone()

    if user:
        return jsonify({'user_id': user[0], 'name': user[1], 'email': user[2]})
    else:
        return jsonify({'message': 'User not found'}), 404

@app.route('/users/<int:user_id>', methods=['PUT'])
def update_user(user_id):
    name = request.json['name']
    email = request.json['email']

    cursor.execute("UPDATE users SET name = %s, email = %s WHERE user_id = %s", (name, email, user_id))
    conn.commit()

    return jsonify({'message': 'User updated successfully'})

@app.route('/users/<int:user_id>', methods=['DELETE'])
def delete_user(user_id):
    cursor.execute("DELETE FROM users WHERE user_id = %s", (user_id,))
```

```
conn.commit()

return jsonify({'message': 'User deleted successfully'})

if __name__ == '__main__':
    app.run(debug=True)
```
```

## Choosing the Right Database

When deciding between DynamoDB and PostgreSQL, consider the following factors:

**1. Data Model:** DynamoDB is ideal for hierarchical data or when the data structure can change over time. PostgreSQL is better suited for relational data with complex relationships.

**2. Query Complexity:** If your application requires complex queries, joins, and transactions, PostgreSQL is the better choice. DynamoDB excels at simple queries and fast read/write operations.

**3. Scalability Needs**: DynamoDB automatically scales with traffic, making it ideal for applications with variable workloads. PostgreSQL can scale, but it often requires more manual intervention and planning.
```

4. Consistency Requirements: PostgreSQL provides strong consistency with ACID properties. DynamoDB offers eventual consistency by default, with the option for strongly consistent reads.

5. Cost: Evaluate the cost implications based on your read/write operations and storage needs. DynamoDB's cost can escalate with high traffic, whereas PostgreSQL may have higher operational costs due to management overhead.

Choosing the right database for your API is a balancing act that depends on your specific application requirements. DynamoDB offers high performance and scalability for applications with simple queries and variable workloads, while PostgreSQL provides robust support for complex queries and strong consistency for relational data.

By understanding the strengths and limitations of each database, you can make an informed decision that aligns with your application's needs. Whether you choose DynamoDB for its scalability or PostgreSQL for its rich query capabilities, the key is to design your API to leverage the chosen database's features effectively, ensuring a robust and scalable solution for your users.

Chapter 2

Unveiling REST: Building User-Friendly APIs

Understanding RESTful Architecture: Core Principles and Design Patterns

In the evolving landscape of web development, RESTful architecture stands out as a pivotal model for designing networked applications. REST, or Representational State Transfer, is an architectural style that provides guidelines and best practices for creating scalable and maintainable web services. Understanding the core principles and design patterns of RESTful architecture is essential for building effective APIs. This article delves into the key concepts of RESTful architecture, and illustrates these principles with practical examples using DynamoDB and PostgreSQL.

What is RESTful Architecture?

REST is an architectural style defined by constraints that ensure a high degree of scalability, simplicity, and performance in web applications. Proposed by Roy Fielding in his doctoral dissertation in 2000, REST has since become the standard for web APIs.

Core Principles of REST

1. Statelessness

In REST, each request from a client to a server must contain all the information needed to understand and process the request. This means the server does not store any client context between requests, making each interaction independent and stateless.

2. Client-Server Architecture

REST is based on a client-server architecture where the client and server operate independently. The client handles the user interface and user experience, while the server manages data storage and business logic. This separation allows for greater scalability and flexibility in development.

3. Uniform Interface

A uniform interface simplifies and decouples the architecture, allowing each part to evolve independently. The uniform interface is fundamental to REST and includes:

- **Resource Identification:** Each resource is identified by a unique URI.

- **Resource Manipulation Through Representations:** Clients interact with resources by using representations (e.g., JSON, XML).

- **Self-descriptive Messages:** Each message contains enough information to describe how to process the message.

- **Hypermedia as the Engine of Application State (HATEOAS):** Clients use hyperlinks to navigate the state of the application dynamically.

4. Layered System

A layered system architecture allows for hierarchical organization, where each layer interacts only with the adjacent layers. This design enhances scalability and security, as layers can be added, modified, or replaced independently.

5. Code on Demand (Optional)

Though optional, servers can extend client functionality by transferring executable code. This can be useful for enhancing client applications dynamically.

Design Patterns in RESTful Architecture

1. Resource-Based Design

In RESTful architecture, everything is treated as a resource. Resources are identified using URIs, and the standard HTTP methods (GET, POST, PUT, DELETE) are used to perform CRUD operations.

2. CRUD Operations

The fundamental operations in RESTful services map directly to the HTTP methods:

- **GET**: Retrieve a resource.
- **POST**: Create a new resource.
- **PUT**: Update an existing resource.
- **DELETE**: Remove a resource.

3. Idempotency

RESTful operations should be idempotent, meaning that multiple identical requests should have the same effect as a single request. GET, PUT, and DELETE are inherently idempotent, while POST is not.

4. Pagination and Filtering

For handling large datasets, RESTful services often implement pagination and filtering. This helps in breaking down the data into manageable chunks and allows clients to request only the data they need.

Building RESTful APIs with DynamoDB

DynamoDB, a NoSQL database service by Amazon Web Services (AWS), is known for its high performance and scalability. We will create a RESTful API for managing user data using Flask and Boto3, AWS's SDK for Python.

Setting Up DynamoDB

First, we need to set up DynamoDB and create a table for users.

```python
import boto3

# Initialize a session using Amazon DynamoDB
dynamodb = boto3.resource('dynamodb', region_name='us-west-2')

# Create the DynamoDB table
```

```
table = dynamodb.create_table(
    TableName='Users',
    KeySchema=[
        {
            'AttributeName': 'user_id',
            'KeyType': 'HASH'  # Partition key
        }
    ],
    AttributeDefinitions=[
        {
            'AttributeName': 'user_id',
            'AttributeType': 'S'
        }
    ],
    ProvisionedThroughput={
        'ReadCapacityUnits': 5,
        'WriteCapacityUnits': 5
    }
)

# Wait until the table exists.
table.meta.client.get_waiter('table_exists').wait(TableName='Users')

print("Table status:", table.table_status)
```
```

## Building the API

Next, we create a Flask application to perform CRUD operations on the DynamoDB table.
```

```python
from flask import Flask, request, jsonify
import boto3
from boto3.dynamodb.conditions import Key

app = Flask(__name__)
dynamodb = boto3.resource('dynamodb', region_name='us-west-2')
table = dynamodb.Table('Users')

@app.route('/users', methods=['POST'])
def create_user():
    user_id = request.json['user_id']
    name = request.json['name']
    email = request.json['email']

    table.put_item(
        Item={
            'user_id': user_id,
            'name': name,
            'email': email
        }
    )
    return jsonify({'message': 'User created successfully'}), 201

@app.route('/users/<user_id>', methods=['GET'])
def get_user(user_id):
```

```python
    response = table.get_item(
        Key={
            'user_id': user_id
        }
    )

    if 'Item' in response:
        return jsonify(response['Item'])
    else:
        return jsonify({'message': 'User not found'}), 404

@app.route('/users/<user_id>', methods=['PUT'])
def update_user(user_id):
    name = request.json['name']
    email = request.json['email']

    table.update_item(
        Key={
            'user_id': user_id
        },
        UpdateExpression="set #n=:n, email=:e",
        ExpressionAttributeValues={
            ':n': name,
            ':e': email
        },
        ExpressionAttributeNames={
            "#n": "name"
        }
```

```
    return jsonify({'message': 'User updated successfully'})

@app.route('/users/<user_id>', methods=['DELETE'])
def delete_user(user_id):
    table.delete_item(
        Key={
            'user_id': user_id
        }
    )
    return jsonify({'message': 'User deleted successfully'})

if __name__ == '__main__':
    app.run(debug=True)
```
```

## Building RESTful APIs with PostgreSQL

PostgreSQL is a powerful, open-source relational database known for its robustness and comprehensive feature set. We will create a similar RESTful API using PostgreSQL.

## Setting Up PostgreSQL

First, install PostgreSQL and create a database and table for users.
```

```sql
CREATE DATABASE userdb;
\c userdb

CREATE TABLE users (
  user_id SERIAL PRIMARY KEY,
  name VARCHAR(100),
  email VARCHAR(100)
);
```

Building the API

We use Flask and `psycopg2`, a PostgreSQL adapter for Python, to create the RESTful API.

```python
from flask import Flask, request, jsonify
import psycopg2

app = Flask(__name__)

conn = psycopg2.connect(
  database="userdb",
  user="yourusername",
  password="yourpassword",
  host="127.0.0.1",
  port="5432"
```

```python
)
cursor = conn.cursor()

@app.route('/users', methods=['POST'])
def create_user():
    name = request.json['name']
    email = request.json['email']

    cursor.execute("INSERT INTO users (name, email) VALUES (%s, %s) RETURNING user_id", (name, email))
    user_id = cursor.fetchone()[0]
    conn.commit()

    return jsonify({'user_id': user_id, 'message': 'User created successfully'}), 201

@app.route('/users/<int:user_id>', methods=['GET'])
def get_user(user_id):
    cursor.execute("SELECT * FROM users WHERE user_id = %s", (user_id,))
    user = cursor.fetchone()

    if user:
        return jsonify({'user_id': user[0], 'name': user[1], 'email': user[2]})
    else:
        return jsonify({'message': 'User not found'}), 404
```

```
@app.route('/users/<int:user_id>', methods=['PUT'])
def update_user(user_id):
    name = request.json['name']
    email = request.json['email']

    cursor.execute("UPDATE users SET name = %s, email = %s WHERE user_id = %s", (name, email, user_id))
    conn.commit()

    return jsonify({'message': 'User updated successfully'})

@app.route('/users/<int:user_id>', methods=['DELETE'])
def delete_user(user_id):
    cursor.execute("DELETE FROM users WHERE user_id = %s", (user_id,))
    conn.commit()

    return jsonify({'message': 'User deleted successfully'})

if __name__ == '__main__':
    app.run(debug=True)
```

Advanced RESTful Design Patterns

1. HATEOAS (Hypermedia as the Engine of Application State)

HATEOAS is a constraint of the REST application architecture that keeps the client decoupled from the server. It allows clients to dynamically navigate to related resources through hyperlinks provided in the responses.

```python
@app.route('/users/<int:user_id>', methods=['GET'])
def get_user(user_id):
    cursor.execute("SELECT * FROM users WHERE user_id = %s", (user_id,))
    user = cursor.fetchone()

    if user:
        return jsonify({
           'user_id': user[0],
           'name': user[1],
            'email': user[2],
            'links': {
               'self': f'/users/{user_id}',
               'update': f'/users/{user_id}',
               'delete': f'/users/{user_id}'
            }
        })
    else:
```

```
        return jsonify({'message': 'User not found'}), 404
```

2. Pagination

Handling large datasets efficiently requires implementing pagination to break data into manageable chunks. Here's how you can add pagination to your RESTful API using PostgreSQL:

```python
@app.route('/users', methods=['GET'])
def get_users():
    page = int(request.args.get('page', 1))
    per_page = int(request.args.get('per_page', 10))
    offset = (page - 1) * per_page

    cursor.execute("SELECT * FROM users LIMIT %s OFFSET %s", (per_page, offset))
    users = cursor.fetchall()

    cursor.execute("SELECT COUNT(*) FROM users")
    total = cursor.fetchone()[0]

    return jsonify({
        'total': total,
        'page': page,
        'per_page': per_page,
```

```
    'data': [
        {'user_id': user[0], 'name': user[1], 'email': user[2]} for user in users
    ]
```

For DynamoDB, we can implement pagination using the `LastEvaluatedKey` attribute:

```python
@app.route('/users', methods=['GET'])
def get_users():
    last_evaluated_key = request.args.get('last_evaluated_key', None)
    limit = int(request.args.get('limit', 10))

    if last_evaluated_key:
        response = table.scan(Limit=limit, ExclusiveStartKey={'user_id': last_evaluated_key})
    else:
        response = table.scan(Limit=limit)

    users = response.get('Items', [])
    last_evaluated_key = response.get('LastEvaluatedKey', None)

    return jsonify({
        'data': users,
```

```
        'last_evaluated_key': last_evaluated_key
    })
```

Security Best Practices

1. Authentication and Authorization

Implementing authentication and authorization is crucial for securing your API. Using JWT (JSON Web Tokens) is a common practice:

```python
from flask_jwt_extended import JWTManager, create_access_token, jwt_required

app.config['JWT_SECRET_KEY'] = 'your_secret_key'
jwt = JWTManager(app)

@app.route('/login', methods=['POST'])
def login():
    username = request.json['username']
    password = request.json['password']
    # Verify username and password
    access_token = create_access_token(identity=username)
    return jsonify(access_token=access_token)
```

```python
@app.route('/protected', methods=['GET'])
@jwt_required()
def protected():
    return jsonify(logged_in_as=request.json.get('username')), 200
```

2. Input Validation

Always validate input data to prevent SQL injection and other vulnerabilities:

```python
from flask import request
from flask_inputs import Inputs
from flask_inputs.validators import JsonSchema

user_schema = {
    'type': 'object',
    'properties': {
        'name': {'type': 'string'},
        'email': {'type': 'string', 'format': 'email'}
    },
    'required': ['name', 'email']
}

class UserInputs(Inputs):
    json = [JsonSchema(schema=user_schema)]
```

```
@app.route('/users', methods=['POST'])
def create_user():
    inputs = UserInputs(request)
    if not inputs.validate():
        return jsonify(success=False, errors=inputs.errors), 400

    name = request.json['name']
    email = request.json['email']
    # Insert user into the database
```

Caching

Implementing caching can significantly improve the performance of your API. Tools like Redis can be used for this purpose:

```python
import redis

cache = redis.StrictRedis(host='localhost', port=6379, db=0)

@app.route('/users/<int:user_id>', methods=['GET'])
def get_user(user_id):
    cached_user = cache.get(f'user:{user_id}')
```

```
    if cached_user:
        return jsonify(eval(cached_user))

    cursor.execute("SELECT * FROM users WHERE user_id = %s", (user_id,))
    user = cursor.fetchone()

    if user:
        user_data = {'user_id': user[0], 'name': user[1], 'email': user[2]}
        cache.set(f'user:{user_id}', str(user_data))
        return jsonify(user_data)
    else:
        return jsonify({'message': 'User not found'}), 404
```

Logging and Monitoring

Implementing proper logging and monitoring helps in diagnosing issues and understanding usage patterns:

```python
import logging

logging.basicConfig(level=logging.INFO)
logger = logging.getLogger(__name__)

@app.route('/users', methods=['POST'])
```

```
def create_user():
    name = request.json['name']
    email = request.json['email']

    # Insert user into the database
    logger.info(f"User created: {name}, {email}")
    return jsonify({'message': 'User created successfully'}), 201
```

Testing

Writing tests for your API is essential for ensuring its functionality and reliability:

```python
import unittest
from your_flask_app import app

class UserApiTest(unittest.TestCase):
    def setUp(self):
        self.app = app.test_client()
        self.app.testing = True

    def test_create_user(self):
        response = self.app.post('/users', json={'name': 'Test User', 'email': 'test@example.com'})
        self.assertEqual(response.status_code, 201)
```

```
    def test_get_user(self):
        response = self.app.get('/users/1')
        self.assertEqual(response.status_code, 200)
        self.assertIn('name', response.get_json())

if __name__ == '__main__':
    unittest.main()
```

RESTful architecture offers a structured and scalable way to build APIs, ensuring that applications can grow and adapt to changing requirements. By adhering to REST principles—such as statelessness, a uniform interface, and resource-based design—developers can create APIs that are both robust and easy to maintain.

When implementing RESTful APIs, choosing the right database is crucial. DynamoDB provides a scalable and high-performance solution for simple, unstructured data, while PostgreSQL excels in handling complex queries and relational data. Through practical examples with both DynamoDB and PostgreSQL, we have demonstrated how to build RESTful APIs that follow best practices, including pagination, security, caching, and testing.

Ultimately, understanding and applying the core principles and design patterns of RESTful architecture will enable developers to create powerful and efficient APIs that meet the demands of modern applications.

Designing RESTful Endpoints: Crafting Clear and Consistent API Interactions

Designing RESTful endpoints is a critical task in API development that can significantly impact the usability, maintainability, and scalability of your web services. This guide delves into the principles and best practices for designing RESTful endpoints, using practical examples with DynamoDB and PostgreSQL to illustrate the concepts.

Principles of RESTful Endpoint Design

1. Resource-Based Approach

RESTful APIs are centered around resources, which are the key abstractions of information exposed by the service. Each resource is identified by a unique URI (Uniform Resource Identifier).

For example:

- `/users` might represent a collection of user resources.

- `/users/{user_id}` represents a specific user resource.

2. HTTP Methods

Standard HTTP methods are used to perform CRUD (Create, Read, Update, Delete) operations on resources:

- **GET**: Retrieve a resource.

- **POST**: Create a new resource.

- **PUT**: Update an existing resource.

- **DELETE**: Remove a resource.

3. Consistent Naming Conventions

Use clear and consistent naming conventions for your endpoints. Plural nouns are typically used for collections (e.g., `/users`), and singular nouns are used for individual resources (e.g., `/users/{user_id}`).

4. Use of Status Codes

Leverage HTTP status codes to indicate the result of an operation. Commonly used status codes include:

- `200 OK`: The request was successful.

- `201 Created`: A new resource has been created.

- `204 No Content`: The request was successful, but there is no content to return.

- `400 Bad Request`: The request was malformed.

- `404 Not Found`: The requested resource was not found.

- `500 Internal Server Error`: The server encountered an error.

Example: Building RESTful APIs with DynamoDB

DynamoDB, a NoSQL database provided by AWS, is known for its scalability and performance. Let's design and implement RESTful endpoints for managing user data with DynamoDB.

<u>Setting Up DynamoDB</u>

First, set up DynamoDB and create a table for users:

```python
import boto3

# Initialize a session using Amazon DynamoDB
dynamodb = boto3.resource('dynamodb', region_name='us-west-2')

# Create the DynamoDB table
table = dynamodb.create_table(
    TableName='Users',
    KeySchema=[
        {
            'AttributeName': 'user_id',
            'KeyType': 'HASH'  # Partition key
        }
    AttributeDefinitions=[
        {
            'AttributeName': 'user_id',
            'AttributeType': 'S'
        }
    ProvisionedThroughput={
        'ReadCapacityUnits': 5,
        'WriteCapacityUnits': 5
    }

# Wait until the table exists.
```

table.meta.client.get_waiter('table_exists').wait(TableName='Users')

print("Table status:", table.table_status)
```

### Designing Endpoints

Let's design RESTful endpoints for the user resource:

- **GET /users:** Retrieve all users.
- **POST /users:** Create a new user.
- **GET /users/{user_id}:** Retrieve a specific user.
- **PUT /users/{user_id}:** Update a specific user.
- **DELETE /users/{user_id}:** Delete a specific user.

### Implementing the API with Flask and Boto3

We will use Flask to create our RESTful API and Boto3 to interact with DynamoDB.

```python
from flask import Flask, request, jsonify

```
import boto3
from boto3.dynamodb.conditions import Key

app = Flask(__name__)
dynamodb = boto3.resource('dynamodb',
region_name='us-west-2')
table = dynamodb.Table('Users')

@app.route('/users', methods=['GET'])
def get_users():
    response = table.scan()
    users = response.get('Items', [])
    return jsonify(users), 200

@app.route('/users', methods=['POST'])
def create_user():
    user_id = request.json['user_id']
    name = request.json['name']
    email = request.json['email']

    table.put_item(
        Item={
            'user_id': user_id,
            'name': name,
            'email': email
        }
```

```python
    return jsonify({'message': 'User created successfully'}), 201

@app.route('/users/<user_id>', methods=['GET'])
def get_user(user_id):
    response = table.get_item(
        Key={
            'user_id': user_id
        }
    )

    if 'Item' in response:
        return jsonify(response['Item']), 200
    else:
        return jsonify({'message': 'User not found'}), 404

@app.route('/users/<user_id>', methods=['PUT'])
def update_user(user_id):
    name = request.json['name']
    email = request.json['email']

    table.update_item(
        Key={
            'user_id': user_id
        },
        UpdateExpression="set #n=:n, email=:e",
        ExpressionAttributeValues={
            ':n': name,
            ':e': email
```

```
    },
    ExpressionAttributeNames={
        "#n": "name"
    }
    return jsonify({'message': 'User updated
successfully'}), 200

@app.route('/users/<user_id>', methods=['DELETE'])
def delete_user(user_id):
    table.delete_item(
        Key={
            'user_id': user_id
        }
    return jsonify({'message': 'User deleted
successfully'}), 204

if __name__ == '__main__':
    app.run(debug=True)
```

Example: Building RESTful APIs with PostgreSQL

PostgreSQL, a powerful relational database, is known for its robustness and comprehensive feature set. Let's design and implement RESTful endpoints for managing user data with PostgreSQL.

Setting Up PostgreSQL

First, install PostgreSQL and create a database and table for users:

```sql
CREATE DATABASE userdb;
\c userdb

CREATE TABLE users (
  user_id SERIAL PRIMARY KEY,
  name VARCHAR(100),
  email VARCHAR(100)
);
```

Designing Endpoints

The RESTful endpoints for PostgreSQL will be similar to those for DynamoDB:

- **GET /users:** Retrieve all users.

- **POST /users:** Create a new user.

- **GET /users/{user_id}:** Retrieve a specific user.

- **PUT /users/{user_id}:** Update a specific user.

- **DELETE /users/{user_id}:** Delete a specific user.

Implementing the API with Flask and psycopg2

We will use Flask to create our RESTful API and `psycopg2` to interact with PostgreSQL.

```python
from flask import Flask, request, jsonify
import psycopg2

app = Flask(__name__)

conn = psycopg2.connect(
    database="userdb",
    user="yourusername",
    password="yourpassword",
    host="127.0.0.1",
    port="5432"
)
cursor = conn.cursor()

@app.route('/users', methods=['GET'])
def get_users():
    cursor.execute("SELECT * FROM users")
    users = cursor.fetchall()
    return jsonify([
```

```python
        {'user_id': user[0], 'name': user[1], 'email': user[2]}
        for user in users
    ]), 200

@app.route('/users', methods=['POST'])
def create_user():
    name = request.json['name']
    email = request.json['email']

    cursor.execute("INSERT INTO users (name, email) VALUES (%s, %s) RETURNING user_id", (name, email))
    user_id = cursor.fetchone()[0]
    conn.commit()

    return jsonify({'user_id': user_id, 'message': 'User created successfully'}), 201

@app.route('/users/<int:user_id>', methods=['GET'])
def get_user(user_id):
    cursor.execute("SELECT * FROM users WHERE user_id = %s", (user_id,))
    user = cursor.fetchone()

    if user:
        return jsonify({'user_id': user[0], 'name': user[1], 'email': user[2]}), 200
    else:
```

```
    return jsonify({'message': 'User not found'}), 404

@app.route('/users/<int:user_id>', methods=['PUT'])
def update_user(user_id):
    name = request.json['name']
    email = request.json['email']

    cursor.execute("UPDATE users SET name = %s, email = %s WHERE user_id = %s", (name, email, user_id))
    conn.commit()

    return jsonify({'message': 'User updated successfully'}), 200

@app.route('/users/<int:user_id>', methods=['DELETE'])
def delete_user(user_id):
    cursor.execute("DELETE FROM users WHERE user_id = %s", (user_id,))
    conn.commit()

    return jsonify({'message': 'User deleted successfully'}), 204

if __name__ == '__main__':
    app.run(debug=True)
```

Advanced Design Patterns

1. HATEOAS (Hypermedia as the Engine of Application State)

HATEOAS is a REST principle that allows clients to dynamically navigate the API using hyperlinks provided in the responses.

```python
@app.route('/users/<int:user_id>', methods=['GET'])
def get_user(user_id):
    cursor.execute("SELECT * FROM users WHERE user_id = %s", (user_id,))
    user = cursor.fetchone()

    if user:
        return jsonify({
            'user_id': user[0],
            'name': user[1],
            'email': user[2],
            'links': {
                'self': f'/users/{user_id}',
                'update': f'/users/{user_id}',
                'delete': f'/users/{user_id}'
            }
        }), 200
```

```
    else:
        return jsonify({'message': 'User not found'}), 404
```

With HATEOAS, clients can understand how to interact with your API dynamically without needing extensive documentation.

2. Pagination

Handling large datasets efficiently requires implementing pagination. This breaks the data into manageable chunks and is a best practice in API design.

For PostgreSQL:

```python
@app.route('/users', methods=['GET'])
def get_users():
    page = int(request.args.get('page', 1))
    per_page = int(request.args.get('per_page', 10))
    offset = (page - 1) * per_page

    cursor.execute("SELECT * FROM users LIMIT %s OFFSET %s", (per_page, offset))
    users = cursor.fetchall()

    cursor.execute("SELECT COUNT(*) FROM users")
```

80

```
    total = cursor.fetchone()[0]

    return jsonify({
        'total': total,
        'page': page,
        'per_page': per_page,
        'data': [
            {'user_id': user[0], 'name': user[1], 'email': user[2]} for user in users
        ]
    }), 200
```

For DynamoDB:

```python
@app.route('/users', methods=['GET'])
def get_users():
    last_evaluated_key = request.args.get('last_evaluated_key', None)
    limit = int(request.args.get('limit', 10))

    if last_evaluated_key:
        response = table.scan(Limit=limit, ExclusiveStartKey={'user_id': last_evaluated_key})
    else:
        response = table.scan(Limit=limit)
```

```python
    users = response.get('Items', [])
    last_evaluated_key = response.get('LastEvaluatedKey', None)

    return jsonify({
       'data': users,
       'last_evaluated_key': last_evaluated_key
    }), 200
```

Security Best Practices

1. Authentication and Authorization

Using JWT (JSON Web Tokens) is a common practice for securing RESTful APIs.

```python
from flask_jwt_extended import JWTManager, create_access_token, jwt_required

app.config['JWT_SECRET_KEY'] = 'your_secret_key'
jwt = JWTManager(app)

@app.route('/login', methods=['POST'])
def login():
    username = request.json['username']
    password = request.json['password']
```

```python
    # Verify username and password
    access_token = create_access_token(identity=username)
    return jsonify(access_token=access_token), 200

@app.route('/protected', methods=['GET'])
@jwt_required()
def protected():
    return jsonify(logged_in_as=request.json.get('username')), 200
```

2. Input Validation

Validate input data to prevent SQL injection and other vulnerabilities.

```python
from flask_inputs import Inputs
from flask_inputs.validators import JsonSchema

user_schema = {
    'type': 'object',
    'properties': {
        'name': {'type': 'string'},
        'email': {'type': 'string', 'format': 'email'}
    },
    'required': ['name', 'email']
```

```
}
class UserInputs(Inputs):
    json = [JsonSchema(schema=user_schema)]

@app.route('/users', methods=['POST'])
def create_user():
    inputs = UserInputs(request)
    if not inputs.validate():
        return jsonify(success=False, errors=inputs.errors), 400
    name = request.json['name']
    email = request.json['email']
    # Insert user into the database
```

Caching

Implement caching to improve performance, especially for frequently accessed data. Redis is a popular choice for caching.

```python
import redis

cache = redis.StrictRedis(host='localhost', port=6379, db=0)

@app.route('/users/<int:user_id>', methods=['GET'])
```

```python
def get_user(user_id):
    cached_user = cache.get(f'user:{user_id}')
    if cached_user:
        return jsonify(eval(cached_user))

    cursor.execute("SELECT * FROM users WHERE user_id = %s", (user_id,))
    user = cursor.fetchone()

    if user:
        user_data = {'user_id': user[0], 'name': user[1], 'email': user[2]}
        cache.set(f'user:{user_id}', str(user_data))
        return jsonify(user_data), 200
    else:
        return jsonify({'message': 'User not found'}), 404
```

Logging and Monitoring

Logging and monitoring help diagnose issues and understand API usage patterns.

```python
import logging

logging.basicConfig(level=logging.INFO)
logger = logging.getLogger(__name__)
```

```python
@app.route('/users', methods=['POST'])
def create_user():
    name = request.json['name']
    email = request.json['email']

    # Insert user into the database
    logger.info(f"User created: {name}, {email}")
    return jsonify({'message': 'User created successfully'}), 201
```

Testing

Testing is crucial for ensuring the functionality and reliability of your API.

```python
import unittest
from your_flask_app import app

class UserApiTest(unittest.TestCase):
    def setUp(self):
        self.app = app.test_client()
        self.app.testing = True

    def test_create_user(self):
```

```
        response = self.app.post('/users', json={'name': 'Test User', 'email': 'test@example.com'})
        self.assertEqual(response.status_code, 201)

    def test_get_user(self):
        response = self.app.get('/users/1')
        self.assertEqual(response.status_code, 200)
        self.assertIn('name', response.get_json())

if __name__ == '__main__':
    unittest.main()
```

Designing RESTful endpoints requires a thorough understanding of REST principles and best practices. By focusing on a resource-based approach, consistent naming conventions, proper use of HTTP methods and status codes, and advanced patterns like HATEOAS and pagination, you can create APIs that are robust, scalable, and easy to use.

Implementing these principles using technologies like DynamoDB and PostgreSQL shows how versatile RESTful design can be across different types of databases. Ensuring security, caching, logging, monitoring, and thorough testing further enhances the quality and reliability of your APIs.

By following these guidelines, developers can craft clear and consistent API interactions that meet modern application requirements, ensuring a seamless and efficient experience for both developers and users.

Building a Strong Foundation: Tools and Technologies for Building RESTful APIs

In the rapidly evolving landscape of web development, building robust and efficient RESTful APIs is crucial for enabling seamless communication between clients and servers. RESTful APIs are a popular choice due to their simplicity, scalability, and stateless nature, which align well with the needs of modern applications. To build such APIs effectively, leveraging the right tools and technologies is essential. This article will explore the key components and methodologies for building RESTful APIs, focusing on the integration with DynamoDB and PostgreSQL.

Introduction to RESTful APIs

REST (Representational State Transfer) is an architectural style for designing networked applications. It relies on a stateless, client-server, cacheable communications protocol — the HTTP. RESTful APIs conform to the constraints of REST architecture and allow for interaction with RESTful web services. Key principles of REST include:

- **Statelessness**: Each request from a client to a server must contain all the information the server needs to fulfill that request.

- **Client-Server Architecture:** The client and server operate independently, with each responsible for their respective roles.

- **Uniform Interface:** Resources are identified in the requests (typically using URLs) and manipulated using standard HTTP methods like GET, POST, PUT, DELETE.

Choosing the Right Database: DynamoDB and PostgreSQL

When building RESTful APIs, the choice of database can significantly impact the performance and scalability of your application. Two popular options are DynamoDB and PostgreSQL, each offering unique advantages.

DynamoDB

Amazon DynamoDB is a fully managed NoSQL database service that provides fast and predictable performance with seamless scalability. It is ideal for applications that require low latency and flexible schema design. DynamoDB's features include:

- **Scalability**: Automatically scales throughput capacity to meet demand.

- **Performance**: Provides single-digit millisecond response times.

- **Fully Managed:** Handles database maintenance, backups, and replication.

PostgreSQL

PostgreSQL is a powerful, open-source relational database management system known for its robustness and feature-rich capabilities. It is suitable for complex queries and transactional applications. Key features of PostgreSQL include:

- **ACID Compliance:** Ensures reliability and data integrity.

- **Rich SQL Support:** Extensive support for SQL standards and advanced querying.

- **Extensibility**: Supports custom functions and types, making it highly customizable.

Building RESTful APIs with DynamoDB

Setting Up DynamoDB

To get started with DynamoDB, you'll need an AWS account. Using the AWS Management Console, you can create a new DynamoDB table. For example, let's create a table called `Users` with `userId` as the primary key.

```python
import boto3

# Initialize a session using Amazon DynamoDB
dynamodb = boto3.resource('dynamodb',
    region_name='us-west-2')

# Create the DynamoDB table.
table = dynamodb.create_table(
    TableName='Users',
    KeySchema=[
        {
            'AttributeName': 'userId',
            'KeyType': 'HASH'  # Partition key
        }
```

```
    AttributeDefinitions=[
        {
            'AttributeName': 'userId',
            'AttributeType': 'S'
        }
    ProvisionedThroughput={
        'ReadCapacityUnits': 5,
        'WriteCapacityUnits': 5
    }

# Wait until the table exists.
table.meta.client.get_waiter('table_exists').wait(TableName='Users')

print("Table status:", table.table_status)
```

Creating a RESTful API with Flask and DynamoDB

Next, we'll create a RESTful API using Flask, a lightweight WSGI web application framework in Python. Flask is ideal for building APIs due to its simplicity and flexibility.

First, install Flask and Boto3:

```sh
pip install Flask boto3
```

```

Now, create a basic Flask application to interact with DynamoDB:

```python
from flask import Flask, request, jsonify
import boto3

app = Flask(__name__)

# Initialize DynamoDB resource
dynamodb = boto3.resource('dynamodb', region_name='us-west-2')
table = dynamodb.Table('Users')

@app.route('/users', methods=['POST'])
def create_user():
    user_id = request.json['userId']
    name = request.json['name']
    email = request.json['email']

    response = table.put_item(
        Item={
            'userId': user_id,
            'name': name,
            'email': email
        }
```
```

```python
    return jsonify(response)

@app.route('/users/<user_id>', methods=['GET'])
def get_user(user_id):
    response = table.get_item(
        Key={
            'userId': user_id
        }
    )
    item = response.get('Item')
    if not item:
        return jsonify({'error': 'User not found'}), 404
    return jsonify(item)

@app.route('/users/<user_id>', methods=['PUT'])
def update_user(user_id):
    name = request.json['name']
    email = request.json['email']

    response = table.update_item(
        Key={
            'userId': user_id
        },
        UpdateExpression='SET name = :name, email = :email',
        ExpressionAttributeValues={
            ':name': name,
            ':email': email
        },
```

```
      ReturnValues='UPDATED_NEW'
   )
   return jsonify(response)

@app.route('/users/<user_id>', methods=['DELETE'])
def delete_user(user_id):
   response = table.delete_item(
      Key={
         'userId': user_id
      }
   )
   return jsonify(response)

if __name__ == '__main__':
   app.run(debug=True)
```

Explanation of the Code

- **Creating Users:** The `create_user` endpoint handles POST requests to add new users to the DynamoDB table. It expects a JSON payload with `userId`, `name`, and `email`.

- **Retrieving Users:** The `get_user` endpoint handles GET requests to fetch user details based on `userId`.

- **Updating Users:** The `update_user` endpoint handles PUT requests to update user information.

- **Deleting Users:** The `delete_user` endpoint handles DELETE requests to remove users from the table.

Building RESTful APIs with PostgreSQL

Setting Up PostgreSQL

To set up PostgreSQL, you'll need to install PostgreSQL and a Python library to interact with it, such as `psycopg2`.

```sh
sudo apt-get install postgresql postgresql-contrib
pip install psycopg2
```

Next, create a PostgreSQL database and a `users` table:

```sql
CREATE DATABASE mydatabase;
\c mydatabase

CREATE TABLE users (
  user_id SERIAL PRIMARY KEY,
```

```
    name VARCHAR(100),
    email VARCHAR(100)
);
```

Creating a RESTful API with Flask and PostgreSQL

Now, let's create a RESTful API using Flask and PostgreSQL.

First, install the necessary packages:

```sh
pip install Flask psycopg2-binary
```

Create a Flask application to interact with PostgreSQL:

```python
from flask import Flask, request, jsonify
import psycopg2

app = Flask(__name__)

# Database connection
def get_db_connection():
    conn = psycopg2.connect(
        dbname='mydatabase',
```

```python
        user='youruser',
        password='yourpassword',
        host='localhost'
    )
    return conn

@app.route('/users', methods=['POST'])
def create_user():
    name = request.json['name']
    email = request.json['email']
    conn = get_db_connection()
    cur = conn.cursor()
    cur.execute('INSERT INTO users (name, email) VALUES (%s, %s) RETURNING user_id;', (name, email))
    user_id = cur.fetchone()[0]
    conn.commit()
    cur.close()
    conn.close()
    return jsonify({'user_id': user_id})

@app.route('/users/<int:user_id>', methods=['GET'])
def get_user(user_id):
    conn = get_db_connection()
    cur = conn.cursor()
    cur.execute('SELECT * FROM users WHERE user_id = %s;', (user_id,))
    user = cur.fetchone()
```

```python
    cur.close()
    conn.close()
    if user is None:
        return jsonify({'error': 'User not found'}), 404
    return jsonify({'user_id': user[0], 'name': user[1], 'email': user[2]})

@app.route('/users/<int:user_id>', methods=['PUT'])
def update_user(user_id):
    name = request.json['name']
    email = request.json['email']
    conn = get_db_connection()
    cur = conn.cursor()
    cur.execute('UPDATE users SET name = %s, email = %s WHERE user_id = %s;', (name, email, user_id))
    conn.commit()
    cur.close()
    conn.close()
    return jsonify({'message': 'User updated'})

@app.route('/users/<int:user_id>', methods=['DELETE'])
def delete_user(user_id):
    conn = get_db_connection()
    cur = conn.cursor()
    cur.execute('DELETE FROM users WHERE user_id = %s;', (user_id,))
    conn.commit()
```

```
        cur.close()
        conn.close()
        return jsonify({'message': 'User deleted'})

if __name__ == '__main__':
    app.run(debug=True)
```

Explanation of the Code

- **Database Connection:** The `get_db_connection` function establishes a connection to the PostgreSQL database.

- **Creating Users:** The `create_user` endpoint handles POST requests to insert new users into the PostgreSQL table.

- **Retrieving Users:** The `get_user` endpoint handles GET requests to fetch user details based on `user_id`.

- **Updating Users:** The `update_user` endpoint handles PUT requests to update user information.

- **Deleting Users:** The `delete_user` endpoint handles DELETE requests to remove users from the PostgreSQL table based on `user_id`.

Combining DynamoDB and PostgreSQL

In some scenarios, you may want to leverage both DynamoDB and PostgreSQL within the same application. This could be beneficial for hybrid data needs where you utilize DynamoDB for high-speed, scalable storage and PostgreSQL for relational data with complex querying.

Setting Up the Hybrid System

To set up a hybrid system, you would need to configure both DynamoDB and PostgreSQL as demonstrated in the previous sections. Here's an example structure where user profile metadata is stored in PostgreSQL and user activity logs in DynamoDB.

Flask Application with Hybrid Data Storage

First, ensure both databases are properly configured. Then, integrate both databases into a single Flask application:

```python
from flask import Flask, request, jsonify
import boto3
import psycopg2
```

```python
app = Flask(__name__)

# Initialize DynamoDB resource
dynamodb = boto3.resource('dynamodb', region_name='us-west-2')
activity_table = dynamodb.Table('UserActivity')

# PostgreSQL database connection
def get_db_connection():
    conn = psycopg2.connect(
        dbname='mydatabase',
        user='youruser',
        password='yourpassword',
        host='localhost'
    )
    return conn

@app.route('/users', methods=['POST'])
def create_user():
    name = request.json['name']
    email = request.json['email']
    conn = get_db_connection()
    cur = conn.cursor()
    cur.execute('INSERT INTO users (name, email) VALUES (%s, %s) RETURNING user_id;', (name, email))
    user_id = cur.fetchone()[0]
```

```python
    conn.commit()
    cur.close()
    conn.close()
    return jsonify({'user_id': user_id})

@app.route('/users/<int:user_id>', methods=['GET'])
def get_user(user_id):
    conn = get_db_connection()
    cur = conn.cursor()
    cur.execute('SELECT * FROM users WHERE user_id = %s;', (user_id,))
    user = cur.fetchone()
    cur.close()
    conn.close()
    if user is None:
        return jsonify({'error': 'User not found'}), 404
    return jsonify({'user_id': user[0], 'name': user[1], 'email': user[2]})

@app.route('/users/<int:user_id>/activity', methods=['POST'])
def log_user_activity(user_id):
    activity = request.json['activity']
    timestamp = request.json['timestamp']
    response = activity_table.put_item(
        Item={
            'userId': str(user_id),
            'timestamp': timestamp,
```

```python
        'activity': activity
    }
    return jsonify(response)

@app.route('/users/<int:user_id>/activity', methods=['GET'])
def get_user_activity(user_id):
    response = activity_table.query(

KeyConditionExpression=boto3.dynamodb.conditions.Key('userId').eq(str(user_id))
    )
    items = response.get('Items', [])
    return jsonify(items)

@app.route('/users/<int:user_id>', methods=['PUT'])
def update_user(user_id):
    name = request.json['name']
    email = request.json['email']
    conn = get_db_connection()
    cur = conn.cursor()
    cur.execute('UPDATE users SET name = %s, email = %s WHERE user_id = %s;', (name, email, user_id))
    conn.commit()
    cur.close()
    conn.close()
    return jsonify({'message': 'User updated'})
```

```
@app.route('/users/<int:user_id>',
methods=['DELETE'])
def delete_user(user_id):
    conn = get_db_connection()
    cur = conn.cursor()
    cur.execute('DELETE FROM users WHERE user_id = %s;', (user_id,))
    conn.commit()
    cur.close()
    conn.close()
    response = activity_table.delete_item(
        Key={
            'userId': str(user_id)
        }
    return jsonify(response)

if __name__ == '__main__':
    app.run(debug=True)
```

Explanation of the Hybrid Approach

- **User Creation:** The `create_user` endpoint stores user profiles in PostgreSQL.

- **User Activity Logging:** The `log_user_activity` endpoint logs user activities in DynamoDB, providing scalable storage for potentially high-volume activity data.

- **Fetching User Profiles:** The `get_user` endpoint retrieves user profile details from PostgreSQL.

- **Fetching User Activities:** The `get_user_activity` endpoint fetches user activities from DynamoDB.

- **Updating User Profiles:** The `update_user` endpoint updates user profile details in PostgreSQL.

- **Deleting Users:** The `delete_user` endpoint deletes user profiles from PostgreSQL and user activities from DynamoDB.

Best Practices for Building RESTful APIs

Building robust and maintainable RESTful APIs involves adhering to certain best practices:

1. Use Consistent Naming Conventions: Use nouns to represent resources and avoid verbs. For example, use `/users` instead of `/getUsers`.

2. HTTP Methods: Use appropriate HTTP methods for CRUD operations:

- `GET` for retrieving resources.
- `POST` for creating resources.
- `PUT` for updating resources.
- `DELETE` for deleting resources.

3. Status Codes: Use standard HTTP status codes to indicate the result of the API request:

- `200 OK` for successful requests.
- `201 Created` for successful creation of resources.
- `204 No Content` for successful deletion without returning a body.
- `400 Bad Requests` for invalid requests.
- `404 Not Found` for non-existent resources.

4. Versioning: Include versioning in your API URLs to manage changes and backward compatibility, e.g., `/api/v1/users`.

5. Security: Implement authentication and authorization mechanisms to protect your API. Common approaches include OAuth, JWT (JSON Web Tokens), and API keys.

6. Documentation: Provide comprehensive API documentation using tools like Swagger or Postman to help developers understand how to use your API.

7. Error Handling: Return meaningful error messages and handle exceptions gracefully to provide better insights into what went wrong.

Building RESTful APIs with DynamoDB and PostgreSQL allows developers to leverage the strengths of both databases, combining the scalability and low-latency benefits of DynamoDB with the relational capabilities and complex querying power of PostgreSQL. Using frameworks like Flask makes it straightforward to create, manage, and extend these APIs.

By adhering to best practices and leveraging the right tools and technologies, you can build efficient, scalable, and maintainable RESTful APIs that meet the demands of modern applications. Whether you're dealing with high-velocity data or complex relational data, the combination of DynamoDB and PostgreSQL provides a versatile foundation for your API development.

Chapter 3

Introduction to DynamoDB: A NoSQL Database Built for High Performance

Amazon DynamoDB is a fully managed NoSQL database service provided by Amazon Web Services (AWS). It is designed to deliver fast and predictable performance with seamless scalability. DynamoDB enables developers to offload the administrative burdens of operating and scaling a distributed database so they don't have to worry about hardware provisioning, setup and configuration, replication, software patching, or cluster scaling. Let's delve deeper into the core features, architecture, and practical applications of DynamoDB, especially in the context of building RESTful APIs, and compare it with traditional relational databases like PostgreSQL.

Key Features of DynamoDB

1. Scalability: DynamoDB automatically scales up and down to adjust for capacity and maintain performance. It can handle more than 10 trillion requests per day and support peaks of more than 20 million requests per second.

2. Performance: DynamoDB is optimized for high performance, providing single-digit millisecond response times.

3. Managed Service: Being fully managed, it eliminates the overhead associated with database management tasks such as patching, backup, and recovery.

4. High Availability and Durability: DynamoDB replicates data across multiple AWS regions, ensuring high availability and data durability.

5. Flexible Data Model: Unlike relational databases, DynamoDB supports a flexible schema, allowing each item to have a different number of attributes.

6. Secondary Indexes: DynamoDB supports both global and local secondary indexes to enable efficient querying beyond primary key attributes.

Data Model

DynamoDB's data model comprises tables, items, and attributes. Here's a breakdown:

- **Tables**: Similar to tables in relational databases but with a flexible schema.

- **Items**: Equivalent to rows in relational databases but can have varying attributes.

- **Attributes**: Comparable to columns, but each item can have different attributes.

Core Components

Primary Key: Each item in a table is uniquely identified by a primary key. DynamoDB supports two types of primary keys:

- **Partition Key:** A single attribute that uniquely identifies an item.

- **Composite Key:** A combination of partition key and sort key.

- **Secondary Indexes:** Allow querying the data using attributes other than the primary key.

- **Streams**: Capture changes to items in a DynamoDB table and can be used to trigger events.

Basic CRUD Operations in DynamoDB

Let's look at some basic CRUD (Create, Read, Update, Delete) operations using AWS SDK for JavaScript.

Setting Up DynamoDB

First, ensure you have AWS SDK installed:

```bash
npm install aws-sdk
```

Then, configure the AWS SDK:

```javascript
const AWS = require('aws-sdk');
AWS.config.update({
  region: 'us-west-2',
  accessKeyId: 'your-access-key-id',
  secretAccessKey: 'your-secret-access-key'
});

const dynamoDB = new AWS.DynamoDB();
```

```
const docClient = new AWS.DynamoDB.DocumentClient();
```

Creating a Table

Create a table named `Users` with a primary key `UserId`:

```javascript
const params = {
  TableName: 'Users',
  KeySchema: [
    { AttributeName: 'UserId', KeyType: 'HASH' }  // Partition key
  ],
  AttributeDefinitions: [
    { AttributeName: 'UserId', AttributeType: 'S' }  // S denotes string type
  ],
  ProvisionedThroughput: {
    ReadCapacityUnits: 5,
    WriteCapacityUnits: 5
  }
};

dynamoDB.createTable(params, (err, data) => {
  if (err) {
```

```
    console.error("Unable to create table. Error JSON:",
JSON.stringify(err, null, 2));
  } else {
    console.log("Created table. Table description JSON:",
JSON.stringify(data, null, 2));
});
```

Inserting Data

Insert an item into the `Users` table:

```javascript
const params = {
  TableName: 'Users',
  Item: {
    'UserId': '123',
    'Name': 'John Doe',
    'Email': 'john.doe@example.com'
  }
};

docClient.put(params, (err, data) => {
  if (err) {
    console.error("Unable to add item. Error JSON:",
JSON.stringify(err, null, 2));
  } else {
    console.log("Added item:", JSON.stringify(data, null,
2));
```

});
```

## Reading Data

Retrieve an item from the `Users` table:

```javascript
const params = {
  TableName: 'Users',
  Key: {
    'UserId': '123'
  }
};

docClient.get(params, (err, data) => {
  if (err) {
    console.error("Unable to read item. Error JSON:", JSON.stringify(err, null, 2));
  } else {
    console.log("GetItem succeeded:", JSON.stringify(data, null, 2));
  }
});
```

Updating Data

Update an item in the `Users` table:
```

```javascript
const params = {
  TableName: 'Users',
  Key: {
    'UserId': '123'
  },
  UpdateExpression: 'set Email = :e',
  ExpressionAttributeValues: {
    ':e': 'john.new@example.com'
  },
  ReturnValues: 'UPDATED_NEW'
};

docClient.update(params, (err, data) => {
  if (err) {
    console.error("Unable to update item. Error JSON:", JSON.stringify(err, null, 2));
  } else {
    console.log("UpdateItem succeeded:", JSON.stringify(data, null, 2));
  }
});
```

Deleting Data

Delete an item from the `Users` table:

```javascript
```

```
const params = {
  TableName: 'Users',
  Key: {
    'UserId': '123'
  }
};

docClient.delete(params, (err, data) => {
  if (err) {
    console.error("Unable to delete item. Error JSON:", JSON.stringify(err, null, 2));
  } else {
    console.log("DeleteItem succeeded:", JSON.stringify(data, null, 2));
  }
});
```

Building RESTful API with DynamoDB

Building a RESTful API using DynamoDB involves creating endpoints that handle HTTP requests to perform the CRUD operations on DynamoDB tables. We'll use Node.js with the Express framework for this purpose.

Setting Up Express

First, install Express:

```bash
```

```
npm install express
```

Then, create an `app.js` file:

```javascript
const express = require('express');
const AWS = require('aws-sdk');
const bodyParser = require('body-parser');

AWS.config.update({
  region: 'us-west-2',
  accessKeyId: 'your-access-key-id',
  secretAccessKey: 'your-secret-access-key'
});

const docClient = new AWS.DynamoDB.DocumentClient();
const app = express();
app.use(bodyParser.json());

// Create a new user
app.post('/users', (req, res) => {
  const params = {
    TableName: 'Users',
    Item: req.body
  };
```

```javascript
  docClient.put(params, (err, data) => {
    if (err) {
      res.status(500).send("Unable to add item. Error JSON:", JSON.stringify(err, null, 2));
    } else {
      res.status(201).send("Added item:", JSON.stringify(data, null, 2));
    }
  });

// Get a user by ID
app.get('/users/:id', (req, res) => {
  const params = {
    TableName: 'Users',
    Key: {
      'UserId': req.params.id
    }
  };

  docClient.get(params, (err, data) => {
    if (err) {
      res.status(500).send("Unable to read item. Error JSON:", JSON.stringify(err, null, 2));
    } else {
      res.status(200).send(data);
    }
  });

// Update a user
app.put('/users/:id', (req, res) => {
  const params = {
```

```
  TableName: 'Users',
  Key: {
    'UserId': req.params.id
  },
  UpdateExpression: 'set #n = :n, Email = :e',
  ExpressionAttributeNames: { '#n': 'Name' },
  ExpressionAttributeValues: {
    ':n': req.body.Name,
    ':e': req.body.Email
  },
  ReturnValues: 'UPDATED_NEW'
};

  docClient.update(params, (err, data) => {
    if (err) {
      res.status(500).send("Unable to update item. Error JSON:", JSON.stringify(err, null, 2));
    } else {
      res.status(200).send("UpdateItem succeeded:", JSON.stringify(data, null, 2));
    }
  });

// Delete a user
app.delete('/users/:id', (req, res) => {
  const params = {
    TableName: 'Users',
    Key: {
      'UserId': req.params.id
```

```
  }
  docClient.delete(params, (err, data) => {
    if (err) {
      res.status(500).send("Unable to delete item. Error JSON:", JSON.stringify(err, null, 2));
    } else {
      res.status(200).send("DeleteItem succeeded:", JSON.stringify(data, null, 2));
    }
  });
const port = process.env.PORT || 3000;
app.listen(port, () => {
  console.log(`Server running on port ${port}`);
});
```

This code sets up a simple RESTful API with endpoints to create, read, update, and delete users from a DynamoDB table. Each endpoint handles the corresponding HTTP request and interacts with DynamoDB using the AWS SDK.

Comparing DynamoDB with PostgreSQL

While DynamoDB and PostgreSQL are both powerful databases, they differ significantly in their architectures, data models, and suitable use cases.

Architecture

- **DynamoDB**: DynamoDB is a fully managed, NoSQL database service provided by AWS. It is designed for high scalability and low-latency performance. DynamoDB uses a distributed architecture that automatically scales to handle large volumes of data and traffic. It replicates data across multiple availability zones for high availability and durability.

- **PostgreSQL**: PostgreSQL is an open-source relational database management system (RDBMS). It follows a client-server architecture and can be deployed on-premises or in the cloud. PostgreSQL supports ACID (Atomicity, Consistency, Isolation, Durability) transactions and provides robust features for data integrity and relational querying.

Data Model

- **DynamoDB**: DynamoDB is a NoSQL database that uses a key-value and document data model. It stores data in tables, where each item is uniquely identified by a primary key. DynamoDB supports flexible schemas, allowing each item to have different attributes. It is well-suited for applications with rapidly evolving data requirements and large-scale, distributed workloads.

- **PostgreSQL**: PostgreSQL is a relational database that uses a tabular data model. It organizes data into tables with rows and columns, where each column has a defined data type. PostgreSQL enforces schema constraints and supports complex relationships between tables through foreign keys. It is ideal for applications with structured data and complex querying needs.

Use Cases

- **DynamoDB**: DynamoDB is suitable for use cases requiring high scalability, low-latency performance, and flexible data models. It is commonly used in applications such as real-time analytics, gaming leaderboards, session management, and IoT data processing. DynamoDB excels in scenarios where horizontal scaling and seamless integration with other AWS services are essential.

- **PostgreSQL**: PostgreSQL is well-suited for use cases requiring ACID compliance, complex querying, and relational data modeling. It is widely used in applications such as e-commerce platforms, content management systems, financial applications, and data warehousing. PostgreSQL's rich feature set, including support for JSON data types, full-text search, and geospatial queries, makes it versatile for various application domains.

DynamoDB is a powerful NoSQL database service designed for high performance, scalability, and seamless management. It offers a flexible data model, automatic scaling, and low-latency access, making it an excellent choice for modern cloud-native applications. When compared to traditional relational databases like PostgreSQL, DynamoDB excels in scenarios requiring high throughput, dynamic scaling, and simplified administration. However, the choice between DynamoDB and PostgreSQL ultimately depends on the specific requirements and characteristics of the application, including data structure, querying needs, and scalability expectations.

Data Modeling with DynamoDB: Understanding Tables, Primary Keys, and Attributes

Amazon DynamoDB is a fully managed NoSQL database service that provides fast and predictable performance with seamless scalability. It's a great choice for applications that need consistent, single-digit millisecond latency at any scale. When building RESTful APIs, DynamoDB offers a flexible data model that can handle various use cases. In this article, we'll explore data modeling with DynamoDB by understanding tables, primary keys, and attributes. We'll also compare it with PostgreSQL to highlight the differences between NoSQL and SQL databases in API development.

Tables in DynamoDB

A table in DynamoDB is a collection of data items, and each item is a group of attributes. Unlike traditional relational databases, DynamoDB tables do not have a fixed schema, meaning that each item can have a different number of attributes. However, there are some fundamental components that need to be defined when creating a table:

1. Table Name: The unique identifier for the table.
2. Primary Key: A unique identifier for each item in the table.

Creating a Table

Here's an example of creating a DynamoDB table using AWS SDK for Python (Boto3):

```python
import boto3

# Initialize a session using Amazon DynamoDB
dynamodb = boto3.resource('dynamodb')

# Create a table
table = dynamodb.create_table(
    TableName='Users',
    KeySchema=[
        {
            'AttributeName': 'UserID',
            'KeyType': 'HASH'  # Partition key
        },
            'AttributeName': 'Username',
            'KeyType': 'RANGE'  # Sort key
        }
    AttributeDefinitions=[
        {
            'AttributeName': 'UserID',
            'AttributeType': 'S'  # String
        },

            'AttributeName': 'Username',
            'AttributeType': 'S'  # String
        }
```

```
    ProvisionedThroughput={
       'ReadCapacityUnits': 5,
       'WriteCapacityUnits': 5
    }

# Wait until the table exists.
table.meta.client.get_waiter('table_exists').wait(TableName='Users')

print(f'Table {table.table_name} created successfully')
```
```

In this example, we create a table named `Users` with `UserID` as the partition key and `Username` as the sort key. The `ProvisionedThroughput` parameter specifies the read and write capacity units.

**Primary Keys**

Primary keys in DynamoDB uniquely identify each item in a table. There are two types of primary keys:

**1. Partition Key (HASH):** A simple primary key composed of one attribute. DynamoDB uses the partition key's value to determine the physical location of the data.
```

2. Composite Primary Key (HASH + RANGE): A combination of partition key and sort key. This allows for more complex queries, where items with the same partition key can be queried based on the sort key.

Example of Primary Keys

Simple Primary Key

```python
table = dynamodb.create_table(
  TableName='Books',
  KeySchema=[
    {
      'AttributeName': 'ISBN',
      'KeyType': 'HASH'  # Partition key

  AttributeDefinitions=[
    {
      'AttributeName': 'ISBN',
      'AttributeType': 'S'  # String
    }
  ProvisionedThroughput={
    'ReadCapacityUnits': 5,
    'WriteCapacityUnits': 5
  }
```

In this example, `ISBN` is the partition key, and each item in the `Books` table is uniquely identified by its `ISBN`.

Composite Primary Key

```python
table = dynamodb.create_table(
    TableName='Orders',
    KeySchema=[
        {
            'AttributeName': 'OrderID',
            'KeyType': 'HASH'  # Partition key
        },
            'AttributeName': 'OrderDate',
            'KeyType': 'RANGE'  # Sort key
        }
    AttributeDefinitions=[
        {
            'AttributeName': 'OrderID',
            'AttributeType': 'S'  # String
        },
            'AttributeName': 'OrderDate',
            'AttributeType': 'S'  # String
        }
    ProvisionedThroughput={
        'ReadCapacityUnits': 5,
        'WriteCapacityUnits': 5
```

```
    }
```
```

In this example, `OrderID` is the partition key, and `OrderDate` is the sort key. This allows querying all orders for a specific `OrderID` within a date range.

**Attributes**

Attributes in DynamoDB are similar to columns in a relational database. Each item in a table can have different attributes. There are several types of attributes:

**1. String:** A Unicode string up to 400KB.

**2. Number:** A numeric value, either integer or floating-point.

**3. Binary:** Binary data up to 400KB.

**4. Boolean:** A true or false value.

**5. Null:** A null value.

**6. List:** An ordered list of values.

**7. Map:** A collection of key-value pairs.
```

8. Set: A unique collection of values.

Example of Attributes

```python
response = table.put_item(
  Item={
    'UserID': '123',
    'Username': 'johndoe',
    'Email': 'johndoe@example.com',
    'Age': 30,
    'Address': {
       'Street': '123 Elm St',
       'City': 'Somewhere',
       'State': 'CA',
       'ZipCode': '12345'
    },
    'Hobbies': ['Reading', 'Hiking', 'Gaming']
  }
```

In this example, an item with various attributes (string, number, map, and list) is inserted into the `Users` table.

Querying Data

Query Operation

The query operation finds items in a table using only the primary key attributes. You must specify the partition key and can optionally provide a sort key to refine the results.

```python
response = table.query(
    KeyConditionExpression=Key('UserID').eq('123')
)

for item in response['Items']:
    print(item)
```

In this example, the query retrieves all items with `UserID` equal to `123`.

Scan Operation

The scan operation examines every item in the table. It's less efficient than the query operation but allows filtering based on non-key attributes.

```python
response = table.scan(
    FilterExpression=Attr('Age').gt(25)
)
```

```
for item in response['Items']:
    print(item)
```

In this example, the scan retrieves all items where the `Age` attribute is greater than 25.

Building a RESTful API with DynamoDB

To build a RESTful API with DynamoDB, you typically use a web framework such as Flask or FastAPI in Python. Below is a simple example using Flask.

Flask Application Setup

First, install Flask and Boto3:

```sh
pip install Flask boto3
```

Flask API Code

```python
from flask import Flask, request, jsonify
import boto3
from boto3.dynamodb.conditions import Key
```

```python
app = Flask(__name__)

dynamodb = boto3.resource('dynamodb')
table = dynamodb.Table('Users')

@app.route('/users', methods=['POST'])
def create_user():
    data = request.json
    table.put_item(Item=data)
    return jsonify(data), 201

@app.route('/users/<user_id>', methods=['GET'])
def get_user(user_id):
    response = table.get_item(
        Key={
            'UserID': user_id
        }
    )
    item = response.get('Item')
    if item:
        return jsonify(item)
    else:
        return jsonify({'error': 'User not found'}), 404

@app.route('/users', methods=['GET'])
def get_users():
    response = table.scan()
    items = response.get('Items', [])
    return jsonify(items)
```

```
@app.route('/users/<user_id>', methods=['DELETE'])
def delete_user(user_id):
    table.delete_item(
        Key={
            'UserID': user_id
        }
    return '', 204

if __name__ == '__main__':
    app.run(debug=True)
```

Explanation

- **POST /users:** Creates a new user.

- **GET /users/<user_id>:** Retrieves a user by `UserID`.

- **GET /users:** Retrieves all users.

- **DELETE /users/<user_id>:** Deletes a user by `UserID`.

This simple API demonstrates basic CRUD operations using DynamoDB as the backend database.

Comparing DynamoDB and PostgreSQL

When building RESTful APIs, the choice between DynamoDB and PostgreSQL depends on your application's requirements. Here's a comparison to help understand the differences:

Schema Flexibility

- **DynamoDB**: Schema-less, meaning each item can have different attributes.

- **PostgreSQL**: Schema-based, meaning all rows in a table follow a predefined schema.

Scalability

- **DynamoDB**: Horizontally scalable by design, with automatic sharding and replication.

- **PostgreSQL**: Vertically scalable, with options for read replication and partitioning for horizontal scaling.

Query Language

- **DynamoDB**: Uses its own query language, which is less powerful than SQL but optimized for high performance.

- **PostgreSQL**: Uses SQL, which is very powerful and flexible.

Consistency

- **DynamoDB**: Offers eventual consistency (default) and strong consistency (optional). Eventual consistency means that reads might not immediately reflect the results of a recently completed write, but within a short time, all copies of the data will converge. Strong consistency guarantees that a read immediately reflects all writes that received a successful response.

- **PostgreSQL**: Provides ACID (Atomicity, Consistency, Isolation, Durability) transactions and strong consistency by default, making it a reliable choice for applications that require strong transactional integrity.

Performance

- **DynamoDB**: Designed for high performance and low latency. It's optimized for read and write operations on a massive scale, handling millions of requests per second. Performance is predictable and consistent.

- **PostgreSQL**: Performance can be excellent for a wide range of workloads, but it might require more tuning and optimization as the data volume and query complexity increase. It's suitable for complex queries, joins, and transactions.

Cost

- **DynamoDB**: Pricing is based on throughput capacity (read and write capacity units) and storage. It's pay-as-you-go, which can be cost-effective for large-scale applications with variable workloads.

- **PostgreSQL**: Typically involves licensing fees (for commercial versions) and infrastructure costs. It can be more cost-effective for applications with smaller or more predictable workloads.

Use Cases

- **DynamoDB**: Ideal for applications that require high scalability, low latency, and flexible schema design. Common use cases include gaming, IoT, mobile apps, and real-time data processing.

- **PostgreSQL**: Best suited for applications that require complex queries, joins, and transactions. Common use cases include enterprise applications, financial systems, and any application where data integrity and complex query capabilities are essential.

Data modeling with DynamoDB requires a shift in thinking from traditional relational databases like PostgreSQL. Understanding tables, primary keys, and attributes in DynamoDB is crucial for effective data design and efficient query execution.

Summary of Key Points

- **Tables**: Collections of items, each identified uniquely by a primary key.

- **Primary Keys:** Can be a simple partition key or a composite key (partition + sort key).

- **Attributes**: Flexible and can vary between items; include types like String, Number, Boolean, List, and Map.

- **Querying**: Efficiently retrieve data using `query` and `scan` operations.

- **RESTful API:** Build scalable APIs using frameworks like Flask, leveraging DynamoDB's high performance and flexibility.

Practical Tips

- When designing your DynamoDB tables, carefully choose your primary keys based on access patterns.

- Use composite keys to enable more flexible querying.

- Leverage DynamoDB's ability to handle large volumes of data with low latency for performance-critical applications.

- When transitioning from SQL to NoSQL, focus on understanding how DynamoDB's query mechanisms differ from traditional SQL queries.

Example: Building a RESTful API with PostgreSQL

For comparison, let's briefly outline how a similar RESTful API would look using PostgreSQL.

Setting Up PostgreSQL

First, install Flask and Psycopg2:

```sh
pip install Flask psycopg2-binary
```

Flask API Code with PostgreSQL

```python
from flask import Flask, request, jsonify
import psycopg2

app = Flask(__name__)

# Connect to PostgreSQL
conn = psycopg2.connect(
    dbname='your_database',
    user='your_user',
    password='your_password',
    host='localhost'
)
```

```python
cursor = conn.cursor()

@app.route('/users', methods=['POST'])
def create_user():
    data = request.json
    cursor.execute(
        "INSERT INTO users (user_id, username, email, age, address, hobbies) VALUES (%s, %s, %s, %s, %s, %s)",
        (data['UserID'], data['Username'], data['Email'], data['Age'], data['Address'], data['Hobbies'])
    )
    conn.commit()
    return jsonify(data), 201

@app.route('/users/<user_id>', methods=['GET'])
def get_user(user_id):
    cursor.execute("SELECT * FROM users WHERE user_id = %s", (user_id,))
    user = cursor.fetchone()
    if user:
        return jsonify(user)
    else:
        return jsonify({'error': 'User not found'}), 404

@app.route('/users', methods=['GET'])
def get_users():
    cursor.execute("SELECT * FROM users")
```

```
    users = cursor.fetchall()
    return jsonify(users)

@app.route('/users/<user_id>', methods=['DELETE'])
def delete_user(user_id):
    cursor.execute("DELETE FROM users WHERE user_id = %s", (user_id,))
    conn.commit()
    return '', 204

if __name__ == '__main__':
    app.run(debug=True)
```

PostgreSQL Schema

```sql
CREATE TABLE users (
    user_id VARCHAR(255) PRIMARY KEY,
    username VARCHAR(255) NOT NULL,
    email VARCHAR(255),
    age INTEGER,
    address JSON,
    hobbies TEXT[]
);
```

Explanation

- **POST /users:** Inserts a new user into the PostgreSQL `users` table.

- **GET /users/<user_id>:** Retrieves a user by `user_id`.

- **GET /users:** Retrieves all users.

- **DELETE /users/<user_id>:** Deletes a user by `user_id`.

This example illustrates how similar CRUD operations are implemented in PostgreSQL, with a structured schema and SQL queries.

Final Thoughts

Choosing between DynamoDB and PostgreSQL depends on your specific use case and requirements. DynamoDB's flexible schema, high scalability, and low latency make it an excellent choice for modern, high-performance applications. PostgreSQL's robust querying capabilities, strong transactional consistency, and support for complex relationships make it ideal for applications where data integrity and complex queries are critical.

Understanding the strengths and trade-offs of each database can help you design better data models and build more efficient and scalable applications. Whether you're building a RESTful API or a complex enterprise system, both DynamoDB and PostgreSQL offer powerful tools to meet your needs.

Performing CRUD Operations with DynamoDB: Creating, Reading, Updating, and Deleting Data Effectively

Amazon DynamoDB is a fully managed NoSQL database service that provides fast and predictable performance with seamless scalability. This guide will walk you through performing CRUD (Create, Read, Update, Delete) operations with DynamoDB using AWS SDK for Python (Boto3). We will cover the basic operations, best practices, and code examples for each of these operations.

Prerequisites

Before we start, make sure you have:

1. An AWS account.

2. AWS CLI installed and configured with your AWS credentials.

3. Python installed.

4. Boto3 library installed. You can install it using pip:
   ```bash
   pip install boto3
   ```

Setting Up DynamoDB

First, let's set up DynamoDB. We'll create a DynamoDB table to perform our operations.

Creating a DynamoDB Table

We'll create a table named `Users` with `UserId` as the primary key.

```python
import boto3

# Initialize a session using Amazon DynamoDB
dynamodb = boto3.resource('dynamodb', region_name='us-west-2')

# Create the DynamoDB table
table = dynamodb.create_table(
    TableName='Users',
```

```
    KeySchema=[
        {
            'AttributeName': 'UserId',
            'KeyType': 'HASH'  # Partition key
        }
    AttributeDefinitions=[
        {
            'AttributeName': 'UserId',
            'AttributeType': 'S'
        }
    ProvisionedThroughput={
        'ReadCapacityUnits': 5,
        'WriteCapacityUnits': 5
    }

# Wait until the table exists
table.meta.client.get_waiter('table_exists').wait(TableName='Users')

print("Table status:", table.table_status)
```
```

## Creating Data

Creating (or putting) an item in a DynamoDB table is straightforward.

### Code Example: Creating an Item
```

Let's add a user to the `Users` table.

```python
# Define the table
table = dynamodb.Table('Users')

# Add a user
response = table.put_item(
    Item={
        'UserId': '123',
        'Name': 'John Doe',
        'Email': 'john.doe@example.com',
        'Age': 30
    }
)
print("PutItem succeeded:")
print(response)
```

Reading Data

Reading (or getting) an item from DynamoDB requires specifying the primary key.

Code Example: Reading an Item

Let's fetch the user we just added.

```python
# Get the user
response = table.get_item(
    Key={
        'UserId': '123'
    }
)
item = response.get('Item')

print("GetItem succeeded:")
print(item)
```

Updating Data

Updating an item involves specifying the primary key and the attributes to be updated.

Code Example: Updating an Item

Let's update the email and age of the user.

```python
# Update the user
response = table.update_item(
    Key={
        'UserId': '123'
    },
    UpdateExpression="set Email = :e, Age = :a",
```

```
    ExpressionAttributeValues={
        ':e': 'john.new@example.com',
        ':a': 31
    },
    ReturnValues="UPDATED_NEW"
)

print("UpdateItem succeeded:")
print(response)
```

Deleting Data

Deleting an item requires specifying the primary key.

Code Example: Deleting an Item

Let's delete the user from the `Users` table.

```python
# Delete the user
response = table.delete_item(
    Key={
        'UserId': '123'
    }
)
print("DeleteItem succeeded:")
print(response)
```

Advanced CRUD Operations

While the basic CRUD operations are straightforward, there are more advanced use cases and best practices to consider.

Batch Operations

For bulk data operations, DynamoDB provides batch APIs. These are useful for efficient data loading or processing.

Batch Write

```python
# Batch write items to the table
with table.batch_writer() as batch:
    batch.put_item(Item={'UserId': '124', 'Name': 'Jane Doe', 'Email': 'jane.doe@example.com', 'Age': 28})
    batch.put_item(Item={'UserId': '125', 'Name': 'Jim Beam', 'Email': 'jim.beam@example.com', 'Age': 35})

print("Batch write succeeded")
```

Batch Read

```python
# Batch get items from the table
response = dynamodb.batch_get_item(
    RequestItems={
        'Users': {
            'Keys': [
                {'UserId': '124'},
                {'UserId': '125'}
            ]
        }
    }

print("Batch get succeeded:")
print(response['Responses']['Users'])
```

Querying and Scanning

Querying is used to find items based on primary key values. Scanning is used to examine all the items in a table.

Query Example

```python
# Query items by UserId
response = table.query(

KeyConditionExpression=boto3.dynamodb.conditions.Key('UserId').eq('124')
```

)

```
print("Query succeeded:")
for item in response['Items']:
    print(item)
```

Scan Example

```python
# Scan the entire table
response = table.scan()

print("Scan succeeded:")
for item in response['Items']:
    print(item)
```

Best Practices

1. Use Projections: When performing queries or scans, use projections to only retrieve necessary attributes, reducing read capacity units (RCUs) and improving performance.

2. Indexing: Use secondary indexes to support more complex queries without resorting to scans, which can be expensive and inefficient.

3. Conditional Operations: Utilize conditional expressions to ensure operations like updates and deletes only happen when certain conditions are met, maintaining data integrity.

4. Batch Operations: Use batch operations for bulk inserts and deletes to minimize API calls and improve throughput.

5. Capacity Planning: Monitor and adjust read/write capacity based on usage patterns to ensure efficient and cost-effective operations.

6. Error Handling: Implement robust error handling for all CRUD operations to handle transient errors, retries, and exponential backoff.

Performing CRUD operations with DynamoDB using Boto3 is straightforward but requires understanding of the service's capabilities and best practices to use it effectively. By leveraging DynamoDB's features such as batch operations, indexing, and conditional expressions, you can build scalable and efficient applications.

Here's a summary of what we covered:

1. Creating a Table: How to set up a DynamoDB table.

2. Creating Data: Adding an item to the table.

3. Reading Data: Fetching an item from the table.

4. Updating Data: Modifying an item in the table.

5. Deleting Data: Removing an item from the table.

6. Advanced Operations: Batch operations, querying, and scanning.

7. Best Practices: Tips for optimizing your DynamoDB usage.

By following these guidelines and examples, you'll be able to effectively perform CRUD operations with DynamoDB in your Python applications, ensuring both performance and reliability.

Scaling with Confidence: DynamoDB's Auto-Scaling and Partitioning Strategies

Amazon DynamoDB is a fully managed NoSQL database service designed to provide low-latency performance at any scale. Its auto-scaling and partitioning strategies are crucial for ensuring seamless performance as your application's demand grows. This article delves into how DynamoDB's auto-scaling and partitioning strategies work and how to effectively build a RESTful API leveraging DynamoDB and PostgreSQL.

DynamoDB Auto-Scaling

What is Auto-Scaling?

Auto-scaling in DynamoDB dynamically adjusts the provisioned read and write capacity to accommodate changing workloads. It helps maintain application performance while minimizing costs by scaling resources up or down as needed.

How Auto-Scaling Works

1. Scaling Policies: Auto-scaling uses policies to define how and when to adjust capacity. These policies include target utilization, minimum and maximum capacity limits.

2. CloudWatch Alarms: AWS CloudWatch monitors the metrics and triggers scaling actions based on the defined policies.

3. Thresholds: You set thresholds for CPU utilization, read/write capacity units, and other metrics to trigger scaling actions.

Setting Up Auto-Scaling

To enable auto-scaling for a DynamoDB table, you can use the AWS Management Console, AWS CLI, or Boto3. Here's an example using Boto3:

```python
import boto3

# Initialize a session using Amazon DynamoDB
dynamodb = boto3.client('dynamodb', region_name='us-west-2')

# Define the scaling policy
response = dynamodb.update_table(
    TableName='Users',
    ProvisionedThroughput={
        'ReadCapacityUnits': 5,
        'WriteCapacityUnits': 5
    },
    GlobalSecondaryIndexUpdates=[
        {
            'Update': {
                'IndexName': 'index_name',
                'ProvisionedThroughput': {
                    'ReadCapacityUnits': 5,
                    'WriteCapacityUnits': 5
```

}
```

```
print("Auto-scaling enabled:", response)
```

Monitoring Auto-Scaling

Use CloudWatch to monitor auto-scaling activities. Create dashboards and alarms to keep an eye on your DynamoDB table's performance and scaling actions.

```python
import boto3

cloudwatch = boto3.client('cloudwatch', region_name='us-west-2')

response = cloudwatch.put_metric_alarm(
    AlarmName='DynamoDBReadCapacityAlarm',
    MetricName='ConsumedReadCapacityUnits',
    Namespace='AWS/DynamoDB',
    Statistic='Average',
    Period=60,
    EvaluationPeriods=1,
    Threshold=80.0,
    ComparisonOperator='GreaterThanOrEqualToThreshold',
```
```

```
    Dimensions=[
        {
            'Name': 'TableName',
            'Value': 'Users'
        }
    AlarmActions=[
        'arn:aws:sns:us-west-2:123456789012:MyTopic'
    ]
print("CloudWatch Alarm created:", response)
```
```

## Partitioning Strategies

### How Partitioning Works

DynamoDB uses partitioning to distribute data across multiple servers automatically. Each partition can handle a subset of the total data and workload, ensuring that performance remains consistent even as the dataset grows.

### Factors Affecting Partitioning

**1. Table Size:** DynamoDB splits your data into partitions as the table size grows.
```

2. Throughput Capacity: When you provision more read and write capacity, DynamoDB may create additional partitions to handle the load.

3. Partition Key Design: Choosing the right partition key is critical to evenly distribute your workload across partitions.

Best Practices for Partition Key Design

1. Uniform Distribution: Choose a partition key that ensures an even distribution of read and write operations across partitions.

2. Avoid Hot Partitions: Design your keys to avoid situations where a single partition receives a disproportionate amount of traffic.

3. Composite Keys: Use composite primary keys (partition key + sort key) for more granular control over your data distribution.

Example of Partition Key Design

Consider a table storing user activity logs:

```python
table = dynamodb.create_table(
```

```
    TableName='UserActivity',
    KeySchema=[
        {
            'AttributeName': 'UserId',
            'KeyType': 'HASH'  # Partition key
        },
            'AttributeName': 'Timestamp',
            'KeyType': 'RANGE'  # Sort key
        }
    AttributeDefinitions=[
        {
            'AttributeName': 'UserId',
            'AttributeType': 'S'
        },
            'AttributeName': 'Timestamp',
            'AttributeType': 'N'
        }
    ProvisionedThroughput={
        'ReadCapacityUnits': 5,
        'WriteCapacityUnits': 5
    }
```

Building RESTful APIs with DynamoDB and PostgreSQL

Combining DynamoDB and PostgreSQL

Using DynamoDB for high-frequency operations and PostgreSQL for complex relational queries can be a powerful strategy. DynamoDB handles the high-volume, low-latency reads and writes, while PostgreSQL manages transactions requiring ACID compliance.

Setting Up PostgreSQL

First, set up a PostgreSQL database. You can use Amazon RDS for a managed solution.

```sql
CREATE TABLE users (
    id SERIAL PRIMARY KEY,
    username VARCHAR(50) NOT NULL,
    email VARCHAR(100) NOT NULL UNIQUE
);
```

RESTful API Design

We'll design a simple RESTful API with endpoints to create, read, update, and delete users using Flask, a Python web framework.

Flask Setup

Install Flask and Psycopg2 for PostgreSQL interaction:

```bash
pip install flask psycopg2-binary boto3
```

Creating the Flask Application

Setting Up Flask

```python
from flask import Flask, request, jsonify
import boto3
import psycopg2

app = Flask(__name__)

# Initialize DynamoDB and PostgreSQL clients
dynamodb = boto3.resource('dynamodb', region_name='us-west-2')
table = dynamodb.Table('Users')

conn = psycopg2.connect(
    dbname='yourdbname',
    user='yourusername',
    password='yourpassword',
    host='yourhost'
)
cur = conn.cursor()
```

```python
@app.route('/users', methods=['POST'])
def create_user():
    data = request.get_json()
    table.put_item(Item=data)
    cur.execute("INSERT INTO users (username, email) VALUES (%s, %s)", (data['Name'], data['Email']))
    conn.commit()
    return jsonify({'message': 'User created'}), 201

@app.route('/users/<string:user_id>', methods=['GET'])
def get_user(user_id):
    response = table.get_item(Key={'UserId': user_id})
    item = response.get('Item')
    if not item:
        return jsonify({'error': 'User not found'}), 404
    return jsonify(item)

@app.route('/users/<string:user_id>', methods=['PUT'])
def update_user(user_id):
    data = request.get_json()
    table.update_item(
        Key={'UserId': user_id},
        UpdateExpression="set Email = :e, Age = :a",
        ExpressionAttributeValues={
            ':e': data['Email'],
            ':a': data['Age']
        },
```

```
        ReturnValues="UPDATED_NEW"
    )
    cur.execute("UPDATE users SET email = %s WHERE id = %s", (data['Email'], user_id))
    conn.commit()
    return jsonify({'message': 'User updated'})

@app.route('/users/<string:user_id>', methods=['DELETE'])
def delete_user(user_id):
    table.delete_item(Key={'UserId': user_id})
    cur.execute("DELETE FROM users WHERE id = %s", (user_id,))
    conn.commit()
    return jsonify({'message': 'User deleted'})

if __name__ == '__main__':
    app.run(debug=True)
```

Running the Flask Application

Run the Flask application:

```bash
python app.py
```

Testing the API

Use `curl` or a tool like Postman to test the endpoints:

```bash
# Create a user
curl -X POST -H "Content-Type: application/json" -d '{"UserId": "1", "Name": "John Doe", "Email": "john.doe@example.com", "Age": 30}' http://127.0.0.1:5000/users

# Get a user
curl http://127.0.0.1:5000/users/1

# Update a user
curl -X PUT -H "Content-Type: application/json" -d '{"Email": "john.new@example.com", "Age": 31}' http://127.0.0.1:5000/users/1

# Delete a user
curl -X DELETE http://127.0.0.1:5000/users/1
```

Amazon DynamoDB's auto-scaling and partitioning strategies are crucial for maintaining performance and cost-effectiveness as your application's demand grows. By combining DynamoDB with PostgreSQL, you can leverage the strengths of both databases to build robust and scalable applications. This article covered the essentials of setting up auto-scaling and partitioning in DynamoDB, designing effective partition keys, and building a RESTful API with both DynamoDB and PostgreSQL. By following these guidelines and examples, you can scale your application with confidence.

Chapter 4

Introduction to PostgreSQL: A Relational Database for Structured Data Management

PostgreSQL, often simply referred to as Postgres, is a powerful, open-source relational database management system (RDBMS) that has gained widespread popularity for its robustness, extensibility, and standards compliance. Unlike some NoSQL databases like DynamoDB, PostgreSQL is particularly well-suited for applications requiring structured data management, complex queries, and transactional integrity.

In this introduction, we will explore the fundamental concepts of PostgreSQL, compare it briefly with DynamoDB in the context of building RESTful APIs, and provide practical code examples to illustrate its capabilities.

1. PostgreSQL Overview

PostgreSQL has been in active development for over 30 years, making it one of the most mature and reliable RDBMS options available. Key features include:

- **ACID Compliance:** Ensures reliable transactions.

- **Advanced SQL Support:** Comprehensive support for SQL standards.

- **Extensibility**: Supports custom functions, data types, and more.

- **Concurrency**: Efficiently handles multiple concurrent users.

- **Full-text Search:** Built-in full-text search capabilities.

- **JSON Support:** Allows for semi-structured data within a relational framework.

2. PostgreSQL vs. DynamoDB

DynamoDB is a NoSQL database provided by AWS, designed for high scalability and performance with a flexible schema model. In contrast, PostgreSQL follows a fixed schema design, providing a structured and predictable environment ideal for applications with clear relationships and transactional requirements.

Key Comparisons:

- **Schema**: PostgreSQL uses a fixed schema (tables, rows, columns) whereas DynamoDB offers a flexible schema.

- **Query Language:** PostgreSQL uses SQL for queries, while DynamoDB uses a more complex query language that can be limiting for complex queries.

- **Transactions**: PostgreSQL natively supports ACID transactions. DynamoDB offers transactional support, but it's more limited.

- **Scalability**: DynamoDB excels in horizontal scalability. PostgreSQL can scale vertically and, with extensions like Citrus, horizontally.

3. Setting Up PostgreSQL

To start using PostgreSQL, you need to install it on your machine or use a managed service like Amazon RDS.

Installation on Ubuntu:

```bash
sudo apt update
sudo apt install postgresql postgresql-contrib
```

Starting the PostgreSQL Service:

```bash
sudo systemctl start postgresql
sudo systemctl enable postgresql
```

Accessing the PostgreSQL Shell:

```bash
sudo -u postgres psql
```

4. Creating and Managing Databases

In PostgreSQL, you can create a new database and manage tables within it.

Creating a Database:

```sql
CREATE DATABASE mydatabase;
```

Connecting to the Database:

```bash
```

```
psql -d mydatabase
```

Creating a Table:

```sql
CREATE TABLE users (
    id SERIAL PRIMARY KEY,
    name VARCHAR(100),
    email VARCHAR(100) UNIQUE,
    created_at TIMESTAMP DEFAULT CURRENT_TIMESTAMP
);
```

Inserting Data into the Table:

```sql
INSERT INTO users (name, email) VALUES ('John Doe', 'john.doe@example.com');
```

Querying the Table:

```sql
SELECT * FROM users;
```

5. Building RESTful APIs with PostgreSQL

RESTful APIs are a common way to interact with databases over the web. PostgreSQL integrates seamlessly with various frameworks to create robust APIs. For this example, we will use Node.js with the `express` framework and `pg` module for PostgreSQL.

Setting Up a Node.js Project:

```bash
mkdir myapi
cd myapi
npm init -y
npm install express pg
```

Creating the API Server:

```javascript
// index.js
const express = require('express');
const { Pool } = require('pg');

const app = express();
const port = 3000;

// PostgreSQL connection pool
```

```
const pool = new Pool({
  user: 'yourusername',
  host: 'localhost',
  database: 'mydatabase',
  password: 'yourpassword',
  port: 5432,
});

app.use(express.json());

// Get all users
app.get('/users', async (req, res) => {
  try {
    const result = await pool.query('SELECT * FROM users');
    res.json(result.rows);
  } catch (err) {
    console.error(err);
    res.status(500).send('Server Error');
  }
}
// Get a user by ID
app.get('/users/:id', async (req, res) => {
  const { id } = req.params;
  try {
    const result = await pool.query('SELECT * FROM users WHERE id = $1', [id]);
    if (result.rows.length === 0) {
      return res.status(404).send('User not found');
```

    }
    res.json(result.rows[0]);
  } catch (err) {
    console.error(err);
    res.status(500).send('Server Error');
  }

// Create a new user
app.post('/users', async (req, res) => {
  const { name, email } = req.body;
  try {
    const result = await pool.query(
      'INSERT INTO users (name, email) VALUES ($1, $2) RETURNING *',
      [name, email]
    );
    res.status(201).json(result.rows[0]);
  } catch (err) {
    console.error(err);
    res.status(500).send('Server Error');
  }

// Update a user
app.put('/users/:id', async (req, res) => {
  const { id } = req.params;
  const { name, email } = req.body;
  try {
    const result = await pool.query(

```js
      'UPDATE users SET name = $1, email = $2 WHERE id = $3 RETURNING *',
      [name, email, id]
    );
    if (result.rows.length === 0) {
      return res.status(404).send('User not found');
    }
    res.json(result.rows[0]);
  } catch (err) {
    console.error(err);
    res.status(500).send('Server Error');
  }

// Delete a user
app.delete('/users/:id', async (req, res) => {
  const { id } = req.params;
  try {
    const result = await pool.query('DELETE FROM users WHERE id = $1 RETURNING *', [id]);
    if (result.rows.length === 0) {
      return res.status(404).send('User not found');
    }
    res.send('User deleted');
  } catch (err) {
    console.error(err);
    res.status(500).send('Server Error');
  }
```

```
app.listen(port, () => {
  console.log(`Server running on port ${port}`);
});
```

Running the Server:

```bash
node index.js
```

With the server running, you can now interact with the PostgreSQL database using the API endpoints.

PostgreSQL stands out as a versatile and powerful RDBMS, ideal for applications requiring structured data management, complex queries, and transactional integrity. Its compliance with SQL standards, combined with extensibility and robust feature set, makes it a preferred choice for many developers and organizations.

While DynamoDB offers unmatched scalability and a flexible schema for NoSQL applications, PostgreSQL's relational model provides a more structured approach, ensuring data integrity and consistency, which is crucial for many business-critical applications.

By integrating PostgreSQL with modern frameworks like Node.js and using it to build RESTful APIs, developers can leverage its full potential to create scalable, reliable, and maintainable applications. Whether for small projects or large-scale enterprise solutions, PostgreSQL offers the tools and features necessary to manage data effectively.

Creating Powerful Schemas: Defining Tables, Entities, and Relationships in PostgreSQL

In relational database design, the schema is the blueprint that defines the structure of the data. PostgreSQL, as a robust relational database management system (RDBMS), allows developers to create powerful and intricate schemas that define tables, entities, and their relationships in a clear and consistent manner. This is essential for building reliable, maintainable, and scalable applications.

This comprehensive guide will explore the process of creating powerful schemas in PostgreSQL. We'll delve into defining tables, setting up entities, establishing relationships, and incorporating constraints and indices. We'll also touch upon practical examples and provide code snippets to illustrate these concepts, particularly in the context of building RESTful APIs.

1. Introduction to PostgreSQL Schema Design

In PostgreSQL, a schema is a namespace that contains database objects such as tables, views, indexes, sequences, and functions. It helps in organizing and managing these objects within the database. A well-designed schema ensures data integrity, optimizes performance, and simplifies maintenance.

Basic Components of a Schema:

- **Tables**: Store data in rows and columns.

- **Entities**: Represent real-world objects or concepts.

- **Relationships**: Define how entities are related to one another.

- **Constraints**: Enforce rules on data.

- **Indexes**: Enhance query performance.

2. Defining Tables and Entities

Tables are the core components of a PostgreSQL schema. Each table represents an entity and is composed of columns that store attributes of the entity.

Creating a Table:

Let's create a basic `users` table to store user information.

```sql
CREATE TABLE users (
  id SERIAL PRIMARY KEY,
  name VARCHAR(100) NOT NULL,
  email VARCHAR(100) UNIQUE NOT NULL,
  created_at TIMESTAMP DEFAULT CURRENT_TIMESTAMP
);
```

Explanation:

- `id SERIAL PRIMARY KEY`: A unique identifier for each user, automatically incremented.

- `name VARCHAR(100) NOT NULL`: The user's name, which cannot be null.

- `email VARCHAR(100) UNIQUE NOT NULL`: The user's email, which must be unique and cannot be null.

- **`created_at TIMESTAMP DEFAULT CURRENT_TIMESTAMP`:** The timestamp of when the user was created, with a default value of the current time.

3. Establishing Relationships

Relationships define how entities interact with each other. In a relational database, there are three main types of relationships: one-to-one, one-to-many, and many-to-many.

One-to-Many Relationship:

A common relationship type is one-to-many, where one entity is related to multiple instances of another entity. For example, a user can have multiple orders.

Creating `orders` Table:

```sql
CREATE TABLE orders (
  id SERIAL PRIMARY KEY,
  user_id INTEGER NOT NULL REFERENCES users(id),
  product_name VARCHAR(100) NOT NULL,
  quantity INTEGER NOT NULL,
```

```
   order_date TIMESTAMP DEFAULT CURRENT_TIMESTAMP
);
```

Explanation:

- **`user_id INTEGER NOT NULL REFERENCES users(id)`**: Establishes a foreign key relationship with the `users` table, linking each order to a user.

One-to-One Relationship:

In a one-to-one relationship, each instance of an entity is related to a single instance of another entity. For example, a user may have a single profile.

Creating `profiles` Table:

```sql
CREATE TABLE profiles (
   user_id INTEGER PRIMARY KEY REFERENCES users(id),
   bio TEXT,
   profile_picture VARCHAR(255)
);
```

```

**Explanation**:

- **`user_id INTEGER PRIMARY KEY REFERENCES users(id)`**: The primary key is also a foreign key, ensuring a one-to-one relationship with the `users` table.

**Many-to-Many Relationship:**

In a many-to-many relationship, multiple instances of one entity are related to multiple instances of another entity. This is typically implemented using a join table.

**Creating `products` and `orders_products` Tables:**

```sql
CREATE TABLE products (
  id SERIAL PRIMARY KEY,
  name VARCHAR(100) NOT NULL,
  price DECIMAL(10, 2) NOT NULL
);

CREATE TABLE orders_products (
  order_id INTEGER REFERENCES orders(id),
  product_id INTEGER REFERENCES products(id),
  quantity INTEGER NOT NULL,

```
    PRIMARY KEY (order_id, product_id)
);
```

Explanation:

- `orders_products` table links `orders` and `products` with a composite primary key of `order_id` and `product_id`.

4. Constraints and Indexes

Constraints enforce rules on the data to maintain integrity, while indexes improve the performance of database queries.

Adding Constraints:

- **NOT NULL:** Ensures a column cannot have NULL values.

- **UNIQUE**: Ensures all values in a column are unique.

- **PRIMARY KEY:** A unique identifier for records in a table.

- **FOREIGN KEY:** Enforces a relationship between columns of different tables.

- **CHECK**: Ensures values in a column meet specific criteria.

Example with Constraints:

```sql
CREATE TABLE employees (
  id SERIAL PRIMARY KEY,
  name VARCHAR(100) NOT NULL,
  email VARCHAR(100) UNIQUE NOT NULL,
  salary DECIMAL(10, 2) CHECK (salary > 0),
  department_id INTEGER REFERENCES departments(id)
);
```

Adding Indexes:

Indexes are used to speed up the retrieval of rows by creating a data structure that allows for faster searches.

Creating an Index:

```sql
CREATE INDEX idx_users_email ON users(email);
```

```

**Composite Index:**

```sql
CREATE INDEX idx_orders_user_product ON orders_products(user_id, product_id);
```

5. Building RESTful APIs with PostgreSQL

RESTful APIs provide a standardized way to interact with databases over the web. Let's build a simple RESTful API using Node.js, Express, and PostgreSQL.

Setting Up the Environment:

First, initialize a new Node.js project and install necessary dependencies.

```bash
mkdir api
cd api
npm init -y
npm install express pg
```

Connecting to PostgreSQL
```

Create a new file `index.js` and set up the connection to PostgreSQL using the `pg` library.

```javascript
const express = require('express');
const { Pool } = require('pg');

const app = express();
const port = 3000;

const pool = new Pool({
  user: 'yourusername',
  host: 'localhost',
  database: 'yourdatabase',
  password: 'yourpassword',
  port: 5432,
});

app.use(express.json());
```

Defining API Endpoints:

Get All Users:

```javascript
app.get('/users', async (req, res) => {
```

```
try {
  const result = await pool.query('SELECT * FROM users');
  res.json(result.rows);
} catch (err) {
  console.error(err);
  res.status(500).send('Server Error');
}
```

Get User by ID:

```javascript
app.get('/users/:id', async (req, res) => {
  const { id } = req.params;
  try {
    const result = await pool.query('SELECT * FROM users WHERE id = $1', [id]);
    if (result.rows.length === 0) {
      return res.status(404).send('User not found');
    }
    res.json(result.rows[0]);
  } catch (err) {
    console.error(err);
    res.status(500).send('Server Error');
  }
```

Create a New User:

```javascript
app.post('/users', async (req, res) => {
  const { name, email } = req.body;
  try {
    const result = await pool.query(
      'INSERT INTO users (name, email) VALUES ($1, $2) RETURNING *',
      [name, email]
    );
    res.status(201).json(result.rows[0]);
  } catch (err) {
    console.error(err);
    res.status(500).send('Server Error');
  }
```

Update a User:

```javascript
app.put('/users/:id', async (req, res) => {
  const { id } = req.params;
  const { name, email } = req.body;
  try {
    const result = await pool.query(
      'UPDATE users SET name = $1, email = $2 WHERE id = $3 RETURNING *',
```

```
    [name, email, id]
  );
  if (result.rows.length === 0) {
    return res.status(404).send('User not found');
  }
  res.json(result.rows[0]);
} catch (err) {
  console.error(err);
  res.status(500).send('Server Error');
}
```

Delete a User:

```javascript
app.delete('/users/:id', async (req, res) => {
  const { id } = req.params;
  try {
    const result = await pool.query('DELETE FROM users WHERE id = $1 RETURNING *', [id]);
    if (result.rows.length === 0) {
      return res.status(404).send('User not found');
    }
    res.send('User deleted');
  } catch (err) {
    console.error(err);
    res.status(500).send('Server Error');
  }
```

```

### Starting the Server:

```javascript
app.listen(port, () => {
  console.log(`Server running on port ${port}`);
});
```

Running the Server:

```bash
node index.js
```

Creating powerful schemas in PostgreSQL involves defining clear and well-structured tables, establishing meaningful relationships between entities, and enforcing data integrity through constraints and indexes. This process is crucial for building applications that are reliable, maintainable, and scalable.

By integrating PostgreSQL with modern frameworks like Node.js and using it to build RESTful APIs, developers can leverage its full potential to create robust applications. In this continuation, we will delve deeper
```

into advanced schema design practices, practical API development, and performance optimization techniques.

Advanced Schema Design Practices

7. Normalization and Denormalization

- **Normalization**: The process of organizing data to minimize redundancy and improve data integrity. The common normalization forms are:

- **1NF (First Normal Form):** Ensure each table column contains atomic values, and each record is unique.

- **2NF (Second Normal Form):** Meet all 1NF requirements and ensure that all non-key attributes are fully functionally dependent on the primary key.

- **3NF (Third Normal Form):** Meet all 2NF requirements and ensure that all attributes are not transitively dependent on the primary key.

- **Denormalization**: Sometimes, denormalization is used for performance optimization. It involves combining tables or duplicating data to reduce the complexity of queries and improve read performance.

A normalized approach might involve splitting user address information into a separate table:

```sql
CREATE TABLE addresses (
  id SERIAL PRIMARY KEY,
  user_id INTEGER NOT NULL REFERENCES users(id),
  street VARCHAR(100) NOT NULL,
  city VARCHAR(100) NOT NULL,
  state VARCHAR(100) NOT NULL,
  postal_code VARCHAR(20) NOT NULL
);
```

A denormalized approach might combine user and address information in one table:

```sql
ALTER TABLE users
ADD COLUMN street VARCHAR(100),
ADD COLUMN city VARCHAR(100),
ADD COLUMN state VARCHAR(100),
ADD COLUMN postal_code VARCHAR(20);
```

8. Using Advanced Data Types

PostgreSQL supports a variety of advanced data types, which can be useful for specific applications.

- **JSON and JSONB:** Store and query JSON data.

```sql
CREATE TABLE user_data (
  id SERIAL PRIMARY KEY,
  user_id INTEGER NOT NULL REFERENCES users(id),
  data JSONB
);
```

- **Array:** Store arrays of data.

```sql
CREATE TABLE tags (
  id SERIAL PRIMARY KEY,
  name VARCHAR(50) UNIQUE NOT NULL
);

CREATE TABLE post_tags (
  post_id INTEGER REFERENCES posts(id),
  tags INTEGER[] -- Array of tag IDs
```

```
);
```

- **Range Types:** Represent ranges of data.

```sql
CREATE TABLE bookings (
    id SERIAL PRIMARY KEY,
    room_id INTEGER NOT NULL,
    booking_period TSRANGE
);
```

9. Partitioning Tables

Partitioning can improve query performance and manageability by splitting a large table into smaller, more manageable pieces.

Creating a Partitioned Table:

```sql
CREATE TABLE sales (
    id SERIAL PRIMARY KEY,
    sale_date DATE NOT NULL,
    amount DECIMAL(10, 2) NOT NULL
) PARTITION BY RANGE (sale_date);
```

```sql
CREATE TABLE sales_2023 PARTITION OF sales
FOR VALUES FROM ('2023-01-01') TO ('2024-01-01');
```

10. Performance Optimization Techniques

- **Indexing**: Crucial for optimizing query performance.

Example:

```sql
CREATE INDEX idx_users_name ON users(name);
```

- **Query Optimization:** Use EXPLAIN to understand and optimize query execution plans.

```sql
EXPLAIN SELECT * FROM users WHERE name = 'John Doe';
```

- **Vacuuming**: Regular maintenance task to reclaim storage and optimize performance.

```sql
```

```
VACUUM (VERBOSE, ANALYZE);
```

- **Connection Pooling:** Use a connection pool to manage database connections efficiently.

Example in Node.js:

```javascript
const pool = new Pool({
  user: 'yourusername',
  host: 'localhost',
  database: 'yourdatabase',
  password: 'yourpassword',
  port: 5432,
  max: 20, // Maximum number of connections
  idleTimeoutMillis: 30000, // Close idle connections after 30 seconds
});
```

Building Advanced RESTful APIs

11. Handling Relationships in APIs

Fetching Related Data:

When designing APIs, you might need to fetch related data, such as orders for a user.

Example:

```javascript
app.get('/users/:id/orders', async (req, res) => {
  const { id } = req.params;
  try {
    const result = await pool.query(
      'SELECT * FROM orders WHERE user_id = $1',
      [id]
    );
    res.json(result.rows);
  } catch (err) {
    console.error(err);
    res.status(500).send('Server Error');
  }
}
```

Creating Nested Resources:

APIs often require creating nested resources, such as adding an order for a user.

Example:

```javascript
```

```javascript
app.post('/users/:id/orders', async (req, res) => {
  const { id } = req.params;
  const { product_name, quantity } = req.body;
  try {
    const result = await pool.query(
      'INSERT INTO orders (user_id, product_name, quantity) VALUES ($1, $2, $3) RETURNING *',
      [id, product_name, quantity]
    );
    res.status(201).json(result.rows[0]);
  } catch (err) {
    console.error(err);
    res.status(500).send('Server Error');
  }
}
```

12. Using Transactions

Transactions ensure that a series of operations are executed atomically.

Example:

```javascript
app.post('/users/:id/orders', async (req, res) => {
  const client = await pool.connect();
  try {
    await client.query('BEGIN');
```

```
  const { id } = req.params;
  const { product_name, quantity } = req.body;

  const result = await client.query(
   'INSERT INTO orders (user_id, product_name, quantity) VALUES ($1, $2, $3) RETURNING *',
    [id, product_name, quantity]
  );

  // Additional operations can be added here

  await client.query('COMMIT');
  res.status(201).json(result.rows[0]);
 } catch (err) {
  await client.query('ROLLBACK');
  console.error(err);
  res.status(500).send('Server Error');
 } finally {
  client.release();
 }
```

13. Authentication and Authorization

Securing your API involves implementing authentication and authorization mechanisms.

Example with JWT:

```javascript
const jwt = require('jsonwebtoken');
const secretKey = 'yourSecretKey';

app.post('/login', async (req, res) => {
  const { email, password } = req.body;
  try {
    const result = await pool.query('SELECT * FROM users WHERE email = $1', [email]);
    if (result.rows.length === 0 || result.rows[0].password !== password) {
      return res.status(401).send('Invalid credentials');
    }

    const token = jwt.sign({ userId: result.rows[0].id }, secretKey, { expiresIn: '1h' });
    res.json({ token });
  } catch (err) {
    console.error(err);
    res.status(500).send('Server Error');
  }
}
const authenticate = (req, res, next) => {
  const token = req.header('Authorization').replace('Bearer ', '');
  try {
    const decoded = jwt.verify(token, secretKey);
```

```
    req.user = decoded;
    next();
  } catch (err) {
    res.status(401).send('Unauthorized');
  }
app.get('/protected', authenticate, (req, res) => {
  res.send('This is a protected route');
});
```
```

Creating powerful schemas in PostgreSQL involves thoughtful design of tables, entities, and relationships, enforcing constraints, and optimizing performance. By leveraging PostgreSQL's advanced features and best practices, developers can build robust, scalable, and maintainable applications. When combined with modern frameworks like Node.js, these applications can expose RESTful APIs that interact seamlessly with the database, providing a solid foundation for web and mobile applications.

Whether you are normalizing data to maintain integrity, using advanced data types to cater to specific needs, or partitioning tables for better performance, PostgreSQL offers a comprehensive set of tools to manage structured data effectively. By integrating these capabilities into your development workflow, you can ensure that your
```

applications are well-prepared to handle complex data requirements and provide a reliable experience to users.

Performing SQL Operations with Confidence: Crafting Queries for Data Retrieval and Manipulation

SQL (Structured Query Language) is the backbone of relational database management systems like PostgreSQL. Crafting SQL queries with confidence is essential for effectively retrieving and manipulating data, ensuring your applications can provide robust functionality and insightful data analysis. This guide will delve into various SQL operations, providing practical examples and code snippets, particularly in the context of building RESTful APIs with PostgreSQL.

1. Introduction to SQL Operations

SQL operations are broadly categorized into Data Query Language (DQL) and Data Manipulation Language (DML). DQL is used for data retrieval, while DML is used for data manipulation, including inserting, updating, and deleting records.

- **DQL**: `SELECT`

- **DML**: `INSERT`, `UPDATE`, `DELETE`

A well-crafted query ensures efficient data retrieval and manipulation, making your applications faster and more reliable.

2. Data Retrieval with SELECT

The `SELECT` statement is fundamental in SQL, used to fetch data from a database.

Basic SELECT:

```sql
SELECT column1, column2 FROM table_name;
```

Example:

```sql
SELECT name, email FROM users;
```

Filtering Results with WHERE:

The `WHERE` clause is used to filter records based on specific conditions.

```sql
```

```
SELECT name, email FROM users WHERE id = 1;
```

Combining Conditions with AND, OR:

```sql
SELECT name, email FROM users WHERE id = 1
AND email = 'example@example.com';
```

Sorting Results with ORDER BY:

```sql
SELECT name, email FROM users ORDER BY name ASC;
```

Limiting Results with LIMIT:

```sql
SELECT name, email FROM users ORDER BY name ASC LIMIT 10;
```

3. Advanced Data Retrieval

Joining Tables:

Joins are used to combine rows from two or more tables based on related columns.

Inner Join:

```sql
SELECT users.name, orders.product_name
FROM users
INNER JOIN orders ON users.id = orders.user_id;
```

Left Join:

```sql
SELECT users.name, orders.product_name
FROM users
LEFT JOIN orders ON users.id = orders.user_id;
```

Right Join:

```sql
SELECT users.name, orders.product_name
FROM users
RIGHT JOIN orders ON users.id = orders.user_id;
```

Full Outer Join:

```sql
SELECT users.name, orders.product_name
FROM users
FULL OUTER JOIN orders ON users.id = orders.user_id;
```

Aggregating Data:

SQL provides functions to summarize data.

COUNT:

```sql
SELECT COUNT(*) FROM users;
```

SUM:

```sql
SELECT SUM(quantity) FROM orders;
```

AVG:

```sql
SELECT AVG(salary) FROM employees;
```

```

## GROUP BY:

```sql
SELECT department, AVG(salary)
FROM employees
GROUP BY department;
```

HAVING:

```sql
SELECT department, AVG(salary)
FROM employees
GROUP BY department
HAVING AVG(salary) > 50000;
```

4. Data Manipulation

Inserting Data

The `INSERT` statement adds new rows to a table.

```sql
INSERT INTO users (name, email) VALUES ('John Doe', 'john.doe@example.com');
```
```

```

### Inserting Multiple Rows:

```sql
INSERT INTO users (name, email) VALUES
('Alice', 'alice@example.com'),
('Bob', 'bob@example.com');
```

Updating Data

The `UPDATE` statement modifies existing records in a table.

```sql
UPDATE users
SET email = 'john.new@example.com'
WHERE id = 1;
```

Updating Multiple Columns:

```sql
UPDATE users
SET name = 'John New', email = 'john.new@example.com'
WHERE id = 1;

```

Deleting Data

The `DELETE` statement removes rows from a table.

```sql
DELETE FROM users WHERE id = 1;
```

Deleting All Rows:

```sql
DELETE FROM users;
```

5. Transactions and Concurrency Control

Transactions ensure that a series of SQL operations are executed as a single unit of work, maintaining data integrity.

Starting a Transaction:

```sql
BEGIN;
```
```

Committing a Transaction:

```sql
COMMIT;
```

Rolling Back a Transaction:

```sql
ROLLBACK;
```

Example Transaction:

```sql
BEGIN;

UPDATE accounts SET balance = balance - 100 WHERE user_id = 1;
UPDATE accounts SET balance = balance + 100 WHERE user_id = 2;

COMMIT;
```

6. Building RESTful APIs with PostgreSQL

Integrating PostgreSQL with a RESTful API enables you to perform SQL operations through HTTP requests, making data accessible over the web.

Setting Up the Environment:

Initialize a new Node.js project and install necessary dependencies.

```bash
mkdir api
cd api
npm init -y
npm install express pg
```

Connecting to PostgreSQL:

Create a new file `index.js` and set up the connection to PostgreSQL.

```javascript
const express = require('express');
const { Pool } = require('pg');

const app = express();
const port = 3000;
```

```
const pool = new Pool({
  user: 'yourusername',
  host: 'localhost',
  database: 'yourdatabase',
  password: 'yourpassword',
  port: 5432,
});

app.use(express.json());
```

Defining API Endpoints:

Get All Users:

```javascript
app.get('/users', async (req, res) => {
  try {
    const result = await pool.query('SELECT * FROM users');
    res.json(result.rows);
  } catch (err) {
    console.error(err);
    res.status(500).send('Server Error');
  }
```

Get User by ID:

```javascript
app.get('/users/:id', async (req, res) => {
  const { id } = req.params;
  try {
    const result = await pool.query('SELECT * FROM users WHERE id = $1', [id]);
    if (result.rows.length === 0) {
      return res.status(404).send('User not found');
    }
    res.json(result.rows[0]);
  } catch (err) {
    console.error(err);
    res.status(500).send('Server Error');
  }
});
```

Create a New User:

```javascript
app.post('/users', async (req, res) => {
  const { name, email } = req.body;
  try {
    const result = await pool.query(
      'INSERT INTO users (name, email) VALUES ($1, $2) RETURNING *',
      [name, email]
    );
```

```javascript
    res.status(201).json(result.rows[0]);
  } catch (err) {
    console.error(err);
    res.status(500).send('Server Error');
  }
```

Update a User:

```javascript
app.put('/users/:id', async (req, res) => {
  const { id } = req.params;
  const { name, email } = req.body;
  try {
    const result = await pool.query(
      'UPDATE users SET name = $1, email = $2 WHERE id = $3 RETURNING *',
      [name, email, id]
    );
    if (result.rows.length === 0) {
      return res.status(404).send('User not found');
    }
    res.json(result.rows[0]);
  } catch (err) {
    console.error(err);
    res.status(500).send('Server Error');
  }
}
```

Delete a User:

```javascript
app.delete('/users/:id', async (req, res) => {
  const { id } = req.params;
  try {
    const result = await pool.query('DELETE FROM users WHERE id = $1 RETURNING *', [id]);
    if (result.rows.length === 0) {
      return res.status(404).send('User not found');
    }
    res.send('User deleted');
  } catch (err) {
    console.error(err);
    res.status(500).send('Server Error');
  }
}
```

Starting the Server:

```javascript
app.listen(port, () => {
  console.log(`Server running on port ${port}`);
});
```

Running the Server:

```bash
node index.js
```

7. Error Handling and Optimization

Error Handling:

Proper error handling is crucial for building robust APIs.

```javascript
app.use((err, req, res, next) => {
  console.error(err.stack);
  res.status(500).send('Something broke!');
});
```

Optimizing Queries:

Use indexes, optimize SQL queries, and limit data retrieval to improve performance.

Creating Indexes:

```sql
CREATE INDEX idx_users_email ON users(email);
```

```sql
SELECT * FROM users ORDER BY name ASC LIMIT 10 OFFSET 20;
```

Analyzing Query Performance:

```sql
EXPLAIN ANALYZE SELECT * FROM users WHERE email = 'example@example.com';
```

8. Pagination and Filtering in APIs

Implementing pagination and filtering in your API helps manage large datasets efficiently.

Pagination:

```javascript
app.get('/users', async (req, res) => {
  const { page = 1, limit = 10 } = req.query;
  const offset = (page - 1) * limit;
  try { const result = await pool.query('SELECT * FROM users ORDER BY name ASC LIMIT $1 OFFSET $2', [limit, offset]);
    res.json(result.rows);
  } catch (err) {
```

```
    console.error(err);
    res.status(500).send('Server Error');
  }
```

Filtering:

```javascript
app.get('/users', async (req, res) => {
  const { name, email, page = 1, limit = 10 } = req.query;
  const offset = (page - 1) * limit;

  let query = 'SELECT * FROM users WHERE 1=1';
  const params = [];
  let paramIndex = 1;

  if (name) {
    query += ` AND name ILIKE $${paramIndex++}`;
    params.push(`%${name}%`);
  }

  if (email) {
    query += ` AND email ILIKE $${paramIndex++}`;
    params.push(`%${email}%`);
  }

  query += ` ORDER BY name ASC LIMIT $${paramIndex++} OFFSET $${paramIndex}`;
```

```
  params.push(limit, offset);

  try {
    const result = await pool.query(query, params);
    res.json(result.rows);
  } catch (err) {
    console.error(err);
    res.status(500).send('Server Error');
  }
```

9. Securing Your API

Security is paramount in API development. Implementing proper authentication and authorization mechanisms is essential.

JWT Authentication:

```javascript
const jwt = require('jsonwebtoken');
const secretKey = 'yourSecretKey';

// User login
app.post('/login', async (req, res) => {
  const { email, password } = req.body;
  try {
```

```
  const result = await pool.query('SELECT * FROM
users WHERE email = $1', [email]);
  if (result.rows.length === 0 || result.rows[0].password
!== password) {
    return res.status(401).send('Invalid credentials');
  }

  const token = jwt.sign({ userId: result.rows[0].id },
secretKey, { expiresIn: '1h' });
  res.json({ token });
} catch (err) {
  console.error(err);
  res.status(500).send('Server Error');
}
```

```
// Middleware to authenticate requests
const authenticate = (req, res, next) => {
  const token =
req.header('Authorization').replace('Bearer ', '');
  try {
    const decoded = jwt.verify(token, secretKey);
    req.user = decoded;
    next();
  } catch (err) {
    res.status(401).send('Unauthorized');
  }
```

// Example of a protected route

```javascript
app.get('/protected', authenticate, (req, res) => {
  res.send('This is a protected route');
});
```

10. Logging and Monitoring

Implementing logging and monitoring helps in tracking API usage and diagnosing issues.

Basic Logging:

```javascript
app.use((req, res, next) => {
  console.log(`${req.method} ${req.url}`);
  next();
});
```

Using Winston for Advanced Logging:

```javascript
const winston = require('winston');

const logger = winston.createLogger({
  level: 'info',
  format: winston.format.json(),
  transports: [
```

```
    new winston.transports.File({ filename: 'error.log',
level: 'error' }),
    new winston.transports.File({ filename:
'combined.log' })
  ];
};

if (process.env.NODE_ENV !== 'production') {
  logger.add(new winston.transports.Console({
    format: winston.format.simple(),
  }));

app.use((req, res, next) => {
  logger.info(`${req.method} ${req.url}`);
  next();
});
```

11. Testing Your API

Testing ensures your API works correctly and can handle edge cases.

Using Mocha and Chai for Testing:

```bash
npm install mocha chai supertest --save-dev
```

Writing Tests:

Create a new file `test.js`.

```javascript
const request = require('supertest');
const app = require('./index'); // Adjust the path as necessary
const { expect } = require('chai');

describe('GET /users', () => {
  it('should fetch all users', async () => {
    const res = await request(app).get('/users');
    expect(res.status).to.equal(200);
    expect(res.body).to.be.an('array');
  });
});

describe('POST /users', () => {
  it('should create a new user', async () => {
    const res = await request(app)
      .post('/users')
      .send({ name: 'Test User', email: 'test.user@example.com' });
    expect(res.status).to.equal(201);
    expect(res.body).to.have.property('id');
    expect(res.body.name).to.equal('Test User');
```

```
    expect(res.body.email).to.equal('test.user@example.com'
);
  });
```

Running Tests:

```bash
npx mocha test.js
```

Performing SQL operations with confidence involves a deep understanding of how to craft efficient and effective queries for data retrieval and manipulation. From basic data selection to advanced joins and aggregations, mastering these techniques is crucial for building robust applications.

In the context of building RESTful APIs with PostgreSQL, understanding SQL operations allows developers to create powerful and responsive endpoints. The combination of PostgreSQL's robust feature set and Node.js's versatility ensures that applications can scale effectively while maintaining high performance and security.

By leveraging advanced SQL features, optimizing queries, and implementing comprehensive error handling and security measures, developers can create APIs that are not only functional but also efficient and secure. Continuous testing and monitoring further ensure that the API remains reliable and performant as it evolves.

This guide has covered the essentials of SQL operations and their application in API development, providing a foundation for building sophisticated and reliable data-driven applications.

Ensuring Data Integrity: Constraints, Transactions, and Maintaining Data Consistency in PostgreSQL

Ensuring data integrity is crucial for any database system, especially in the context of building RESTful APIs. In this guide, we'll explore how to maintain data integrity using constraints, transactions, and ensuring data consistency in PostgreSQL. We'll draw upon principles from building RESTful APIs with DynamoDB and PostgreSQL to provide a comprehensive approach.

Introduction to Data Integrity

Data integrity ensures that data stored in a database remains accurate, consistent, and reliable throughout its lifecycle. This includes maintaining constraints to enforce rules on data, ensuring transactions are executed atomically, and guaranteeing data consistency across multiple operations.

Constraints in PostgreSQL

PostgreSQL offers various types of constraints to enforce data integrity at the database level. These include:

1. Primary Key Constraint: Ensures that each row in a table is uniquely identified. Example:

```sql
CREATE TABLE users (
  user_id SERIAL PRIMARY KEY,
  username VARCHAR(50) UNIQUE NOT NULL
);
```

2. Foreign Key Constraint: Enforces referential integrity by ensuring that values in a column match values in another table's column. Example:

```sql
CREATE TABLE orders (
  order_id SERIAL PRIMARY KEY,
```

```
    user_id INT REFERENCES users(user_id),
    total_amount NUMERIC NOT NULL
);
```

3. Unique Constraint: Ensures that all values in a column are unique. Example:

```sql
CREATE TABLE products (
    product_id SERIAL PRIMARY KEY,
    product_name VARCHAR(100) UNIQUE NOT NULL,
    price NUMERIC NOT NULL
);
```

4. Check Constraint: Defines a condition that each row must satisfy. Example:

```sql
CREATE TABLE employees (
    employee_id SERIAL PRIMARY KEY,
    age INT CHECK (age >= 18),
    salary NUMERIC CHECK (salary > 0)
);
```

Transactions in PostgreSQL

Transactions in PostgreSQL ensure that a series of database operations are executed atomically. This means either all operations within a transaction are completed successfully, or none are. Example:

```sql
BEGIN;
UPDATE account SET balance = balance - 100 WHERE account_id = 123;
UPDATE account SET balance = balance + 100 WHERE account_id = 456;
COMMIT;
```

If any of the `UPDATE` statements fail, the changes are rolled back, ensuring data consistency.

Maintaining Data Consistency

Maintaining data consistency involves ensuring that data remains accurate and valid, especially when dealing with concurrent transactions or distributed systems. Here are some techniques to achieve this:

1. Isolation Levels: PostgreSQL supports different isolation levels such as `READ COMMITTED`,

`REPEATABLE READ`, and `SERIALIZABLE`. These levels control how transactions interact with each other, minimizing concurrency issues and maintaining data consistency.

2. Locking: PostgreSQL provides various types of locks to control access to data. For example, `ROW EXCLUSIVE` lock ensures that only one transaction can modify a row at a time, preventing concurrent modifications that could lead to inconsistency.

3. Conflict Resolution: In distributed systems, conflicts may arise when multiple nodes try to modify the same data concurrently. Techniques such as optimistic concurrency control or conflict-free replicated data types (CRDTs) can be used to resolve conflicts and maintain data consistency.

Integrating with RESTful APIs

When building RESTful APIs with PostgreSQL, it's essential to ensure that data integrity mechanisms are seamlessly integrated. This involves:

1. Validation: Validate incoming requests to ensure they adhere to database constraints. For example, before inserting data into the database, validate the request payload to ensure it meets the table's schema and constraints.

2. Error Handling: Implement robust error handling mechanisms to deal with constraint violations or transaction failures. Return appropriate HTTP status codes and error messages to the client to communicate the issue effectively.

3. Atomic Operations: Design API endpoints to perform atomic operations whenever possible. For example, if an API endpoint involves multiple database operations, wrap them in a single transaction to ensure atomicity.

Example Integration

Let's consider an example of integrating data integrity mechanisms into a RESTful API built with Node.js, Express, and PostgreSQL:

```javascript
const express = require('express');
const bodyParser = require('body-parser');
const { Pool } = require('pg');

const pool = new Pool({
  user: 'postgres',
```

```js
  host: 'localhost',
  database: 'mydb',
  password: 'password',
  port: 5432,
});

const app = express();
app.use(bodyParser.json());

// Endpoint to create a new user
app.post('/users', async (req, res) => {
  const { username, email } = req.body;
  try {
    const result = await pool.query('INSERT INTO users (username, email) VALUES ($1, $2) RETURNING *', [username, email]);
    res.json(result.rows[0]);
  } catch (error) {
    console.error('Error creating user:', error);
    res.status(500).json({ error: 'An error occurred while creating the user.' });
  }
}

// Endpoint to create a new order
app.post('/orders', async (req, res) => {
  const { user_id, total_amount } = req.body;
  try {
    await pool.query('BEGIN');
```

```
    await pool.query('UPDATE users SET balance = balance - $1 WHERE user_id = $2', [total_amount, user_id]);
    await pool.query('INSERT INTO orders (user_id, total_amount) VALUES ($1, $2)', [user_id, total_amount]);
    await pool.query('COMMIT');
    res.json({ message: 'Order placed successfully.' });
  } catch (error) {
    await pool.query('ROLLBACK');
    console.error('Error placing order:', error);
    res.status(500).json({ error: 'An error occurred while placing the order.' });
  }
}

const PORT = process.env.PORT || 3000;
app.listen(PORT, () => {
  console.log(`Server is running on port ${PORT}`);
});
```

In this example, we've implemented two API endpoints: one for creating users and another for placing orders. We've wrapped the order placement operation in a transaction to ensure atomicity. Additionally, error handling is in place to deal with any failures during the database operations.

Ensuring data integrity is essential for building reliable and robust applications, especially when working with databases like PostgreSQL. By leveraging constraints, transactions, and techniques for maintaining data consistency, developers can build RESTful APIs that handle concurrent operations effectively while preserving the integrity of the underlying data.

Chapter 5

Understanding the Integration Landscape: Choosing the Right Approach for Your Needs

In today's technology-driven world, integrating different systems and databases is crucial for building scalable, efficient, and robust applications. This guide delves into the integration landscape, focusing on choosing the right approach for your needs, particularly when building RESTful APIs with DynamoDB and PostgreSQL.

Integration Landscape Overview

The integration landscape is diverse, encompassing various approaches and technologies. The primary goal is to enable seamless data flow and operation coordination across different systems. Integration can occur at different levels:

1. Database Integration: Connecting and synchronizing data between different databases.

2. Application Integration: Allowing different software applications to communicate and share data.

3. API Integration: Using APIs to enable interaction between disparate systems.

Choosing the Right Integration Approach

Choosing the right integration approach depends on several factors, including data consistency requirements, latency tolerance, scalability needs, and the specific use cases of your application. Here are some common integration approaches:

1. Direct Database Integration

2. API-Based Integration

3. Message Queue-Based Integration

4. Data Streaming Integration

1. Direct Database Integration

Direct database integration involves directly connecting to different databases to perform operations. This approach is often used for real-time data synchronization and ensures immediate consistency.

Example: PostgreSQL to DynamoDB Synchronization

To demonstrate direct database integration, let's consider an example where changes in a PostgreSQL database are synchronized with a DynamoDB table.

Step 1: Setting Up PostgreSQL and DynamoDB

First, ensure you have a PostgreSQL instance and a DynamoDB table ready.

Step 2: Listening to PostgreSQL Changes

We can use PostgreSQL triggers and functions to capture changes and forward them to a script that updates DynamoDB.

```sql
CREATE TABLE users (
  user_id SERIAL PRIMARY KEY,
  username VARCHAR(50) UNIQUE NOT NULL,
  email VARCHAR(100) UNIQUE NOT NULL
);

CREATE OR REPLACE FUNCTION notify_dynamodb() RETURNS TRIGGER AS $$
DECLARE
  record JSON;
BEGIN
  record = row_to_json(NEW);
```

```
    PERFORM pg_notify('dynamodb_channel', record::text);
    RETURN NEW;
END;
$$ LANGUAGE plpgsql;

CREATE TRIGGER user_update
AFTER INSERT OR UPDATE ON users
FOR EACH ROW EXECUTE FUNCTION notify_dynamodb();
```

Step 3: Forwarding Changes to DynamoDB

Create a Node.js script that listens to the PostgreSQL notifications and updates DynamoDB.

```javascript
const { Client } = require('pg');
const AWS = require('aws-sdk');

const dynamoDB = new AWS.DynamoDB.DocumentClient();
const client = new Client({
  user: 'postgres',
  host: 'localhost',
  database: 'mydb',
  password: 'password',
```

```
  port: 5432,
});

client.connect();
client.query('LISTEN dynamodb_channel');

client.on('notification', async (msg) => {
  const data = JSON.parse(msg.payload);
  const params = {
    TableName: 'UsersTable',
    Item: {
      user_id: data.user_id,
      username: data.username,
      email: data.email,
    };
  try {
    await dynamoDB.put(params).promise();
    console.log('Data synced to DynamoDB:', data);
  } catch (error) {
    console.error('Error syncing data to DynamoDB:', error);
});
```
```

## 2. API-Based Integration

API-based integration involves using RESTful APIs to facilitate communication between different systems. This
```

approach is flexible and scalable, allowing systems to interact over HTTP, regardless of their underlying technologies.

Example: Synchronizing Data between a REST API and DynamoDB

Suppose we have a REST API built with Express.js that interacts with a DynamoDB table.

Step 1: Setting Up Express.js and DynamoDB

Ensure you have an Express.js application and a DynamoDB table set up.

Step 2: Implementing the REST API

Create endpoints to handle CRUD operations and interact with DynamoDB.

```javascript
const express = require('express');
const AWS = require('aws-sdk');
const bodyParser = require('body-parser');

const app = express();
const dynamoDB = new AWS.DynamoDB.DocumentClient();
```

```
app.use(bodyParser.json());

app.post('/users', async (req, res) => {
  const { user_id, username, email } = req.body;
  const params = {
    TableName: 'UsersTable',
    Item: { user_id, username, email },
  };
  try {
    await dynamoDB.put(params).promise();
    res.status(201).json({ message: 'User created successfully.' });
  } catch (error) {
    console.error('Error creating user:', error);
    res.status(500).json({ error: 'An error occurred while creating the user.' });
  }
});

app.get('/users/:user_id', async (req, res) => {
  const { user_id } = req.params;
  const params = {
    TableName: 'UsersTable',
    Key: { user_id },
  };
  try {
    const result = await dynamoDB.get(params).promise();
```

```
    if (result.Item) {
      res.json(result.Item);
    } else {
      res.status(404).json({ message: 'User not found.' });
    }
  } catch (error) {
    console.error('Error fetching user:', error);
    res.status(500).json({ error: 'An error occurred while fetching the user.' });
  }
});

const PORT = process.env.PORT || 3000;
app.listen(PORT, () => {
  console.log(`Server is running on port ${PORT}`);
});
```

3. Message Queue-Based Integration

Message queue-based integration uses message brokers like AWS SQS, RabbitMQ, or Kafka to decouple systems and enable asynchronous communication. This approach is ideal for handling high-throughput and fault-tolerant applications.

Example: Using AWS SQS for Decoupling Services

Suppose we have a service that processes user registrations and another service that handles user notifications. We can use AWS SQS to decouple these services.

Step 1: Setting Up AWS SQS

Create an SQS queue for user notifications.

Step 2: Producing Messages

In the user registration service, send a message to the SQS queue after a user registers.

```javascript
const AWS = require('aws-sdk');
const sqs = new AWS.SQS({ region: 'us-east-1' });

const sendMessage = async (user) => {
  const params = {
    QueueUrl: 'https://sqs.us-east-1.amazonaws.com/123456789012/UserNotifications',
    MessageBody: JSON.stringify(user),
  };
  try {
    await sqs.sendMessage(params).promise();
    console.log('Message sent to SQS:', user);
  } catch (error) {
```

```javascript
    console.error('Error sending message to SQS:', error);
};

// Example user registration handler
const registerUser = async (user) => {
  // Save user to the database (not shown)
  await sendMessage(user);
};
```

Step 3: Consuming Messages

In the notification service, poll the SQS queue and process messages.

```javascript
const receiveMessage = async () => {
  const params = {
    QueueUrl: 'https://sqs.us-east-1.amazonaws.com/123456789012/UserNotifications',
    MaxNumberOfMessages: 10,
    WaitTimeSeconds: 20,
  };
  try {
    const data = await sqs.receiveMessage(params).promise();
    if (data.Messages) {
      for (const message of data.Messages) {
```

```
    const user = JSON.parse(message.Body);
    // Process the user notification (not shown)
    await deleteMessage(message.ReceiptHandle);
   }
 } catch (error) {
   console.error('Error receiving messages from SQS:',
error);
 }
};

const deleteMessage = async (receiptHandle) => {
  const params = {
   QueueUrl: 'https://sqs.us-east-1.amazonaws.com/123456789012/UserNotifications',
   ReceiptHandle: receiptHandle,
  };
  try {
   await sqs.deleteMessage(params).promise();
   console.log('Message deleted from SQS');
  } catch (error) {
   console.error('Error deleting message from SQS:',
error);
  }
};

// Poll the queue continuously
setInterval(receiveMessage, 20000);
```

4. Data Streaming Integration

Data streaming integration involves using technologies like Apache Kafka or AWS Kinesis to enable real-time data processing and integration. This approach is suitable for applications requiring real-time analytics and monitoring.

Example: Using Kafka for Real-Time Data Processing

Suppose we have a service that processes user activity logs in real-time.

Step 1: Setting Up Kafka

Ensure you have a Kafka cluster set up.

Step 2: Producing Messages

In the user activity service, send activity logs to a Kafka topic.

```javascript
const { Kafka } = require('kafkajs');

const kafka = new Kafka({
  clientId: 'my-app',
  brokers: ['kafka-broker1:9092', 'kafka-broker2:9092'],
```

```javascript
});

const producer = kafka.producer();

const produceMessage = async (activity) => {
  await producer.connect();
  await producer.send({
    topic: 'user-activity',
    messages: [{ value: JSON.stringify(activity) }],
  });
  await producer.disconnect();
};

// Example user activity handler
const logUserActivity = async (activity) => {
  // Log activity to Kafka
  await produceMessage(activity);
};
```

Step 3: Consuming Messages

In the analytics service, consume activity logs from the Kafka topic.

```javascript
const { Kafka } = require('kafkajs');
const kafka = new Kafka({
```

```
  clientId: 'analytics-service',
  brokers: ['kafka-broker1:9092', 'kafka-broker2:9092'],
});

const consumer = kafka.consumer({ groupId: 'activity-log-group' });

const consumeMessages = async () => {
  await consumer.connect();
  await consumer.subscribe({ topic: 'user-activity', fromBeginning: true });

  await consumer.run({
    eachMessage: async ({ topic, partition, message }) => {
      const activity = JSON.parse(message.value.toString());
      // Process the user activity (e.g., store it in a database, perform real-time analytics)
      console.log(`Received activity: ${activity.type} from user ${activity.userId}`);
    };

consumeMessages().catch((error) => {
  console.error('Error consuming messages from Kafka:', error);
});
```

Integrating with RESTful APIs Using PostgreSQL and DynamoDB

Now that we've discussed various integration approaches, let's look at how you can integrate these concepts into building RESTful APIs using PostgreSQL and DynamoDB.

Designing an API with Multiple Data Stores

When designing an API that uses both PostgreSQL and DynamoDB, it's crucial to define clear boundaries and roles for each data store. For example, PostgreSQL could be used for relational data and transactions, while DynamoDB could be used for scalable, non-relational data storage.

Use Case: User Management and Activity Logging

1. User Management: Store user details in PostgreSQL.

2. Activity Logging: Store user activity logs in DynamoDB.

Step-by-Step Implementation

1. Set Up PostgreSQL for User Management

2. Set Up DynamoDB for Activity Logging

3. Build RESTful API Endpoints

Step 1: Setting Up PostgreSQL for User Management

Create a PostgreSQL table for managing user information.

```sql
CREATE TABLE users (
  user_id SERIAL PRIMARY KEY,
  username VARCHAR(50) UNIQUE NOT NULL,
  email VARCHAR(100) UNIQUE NOT NULL,
  created_at TIMESTAMP DEFAULT CURRENT_TIMESTAMP
);
```

Step 2: Setting Up DynamoDB for Activity Logging

Create a DynamoDB table for logging user activities.

```javascript
const AWS = require('aws-sdk');
const dynamoDB = new AWS.DynamoDB({ region: 'us-east-1' });
```

```
const createTableParams = {
  TableName: 'UserActivity',
  KeySchema: [
    { AttributeName: 'user_id', KeyType: 'HASH' }, // Partition key
    { AttributeName: 'activity_id', KeyType: 'RANGE' } // Sort key
  ],
  AttributeDefinitions: [
    { AttributeName: 'user_id', AttributeType: 'S' },
    { AttributeName: 'activity_id', AttributeType: 'S' }
  ],
  ProvisionedThroughput: {
    ReadCapacityUnits: 5,
    WriteCapacityUnits: 5
  }
};

dynamoDB.createTable(createTableParams, (err, data) => {
  if (err) {
    console.error('Error creating DynamoDB table:', JSON.stringify(err, null, 2));
  } else {
    console.log('DynamoDB table created successfully:', JSON.stringify(data, null, 2));
  }
});
```
```
```

Step 3: Build RESTful API Endpoints

Build RESTful API endpoints to handle user management and activity logging using Express.js.

```javascript
const express = require('express');
const bodyParser = require('body-parser');
const { Pool } = require('pg');
const AWS = require('aws-sdk');
const { v4: uuidv4 } = require('uuid');

const app = express();
const pool = new Pool({
  user: 'postgres',
  host: 'localhost',
  database: 'mydb',
  password: 'password',
  port: 5432,
});

const dynamoDB = new AWS.DynamoDB.DocumentClient();

app.use(bodyParser.json());

// Endpoint to create a new user
```

```javascript
app.post('/users', async (req, res) => {
  const { username, email } = req.body;
  try {
    const result = await pool.query('INSERT INTO users (username, email) VALUES ($1, $2) RETURNING *', [username, email]);
    res.json(result.rows[0]);
  } catch (error) {
    console.error('Error creating user:', error);
    res.status(500).json({ error: 'An error occurred while creating the user.' });
  }
});

// Endpoint to log user activity
app.post('/users/:user_id/activity', async (req, res) => {
  const { user_id } = req.params;
  const { activity_type, description } = req.body;
  const activity_id = uuidv4();

  const params = {
    TableName: 'UserActivity',
    Item: {
      user_id,
      activity_id,
      activity_type,
      description,
      timestamp: new Date().toISOString()
    }
  };
```

```
  try {
    await dynamoDB.put(params).promise();
    res.status(201).json({ message: 'Activity logged successfully.' });
  } catch (error) {
    console.error('Error logging activity:', error);
    res.status(500).json({ error: 'An error occurred while logging the activity.' });
});

// Endpoint to fetch user details
app.get('/users/:user_id', async (req, res) => {
  const { user_id } = req.params;
  try {
    const result = await pool.query('SELECT * FROM users WHERE user_id = $1', [user_id]);
    if (result.rows.length > 0) {
      res.json(result.rows[0]);
    } else {
      res.status(404).json({ message: 'User not found.' });
    }
  } catch (error) {
    console.error('Error fetching user details:', error);
    res.status(500).json({ error: 'An error occurred while fetching user details.' });
});
```

```
// Endpoint to fetch user activities
app.get('/users/:user_id/activity', async (req, res) => {
  const { user_id } = req.params;

  const params = {
    TableName: 'UserActivity',
    KeyConditionExpression: 'user_id = :user_id',
    ExpressionAttributeValues: {
      ':user_id': user_id
    }
  };

  try {
    const data = await dynamoDB.query(params).promise();
    res.json(data.Items);
  } catch (error) {
    console.error('Error fetching user activities:', error);
    res.status(500).json({ error: 'An error occurred while fetching user activities.' });
  }
});

const PORT = process.env.PORT || 3000;
app.listen(PORT, () => {
  console.log(`Server is running on port ${PORT}`);
});
```

Understanding the integration landscape and choosing the right approach for your needs is vital for building efficient, scalable, and robust applications. Whether you opt for direct database integration, API-based integration, message queue-based integration, or data streaming integration, each approach has its strengths and best use cases.

By leveraging the strengths of PostgreSQL for relational data and DynamoDB for scalable, non-relational data, you can design a RESTful API that effectively handles various data management scenarios. With the provided examples, you can start building integrations that ensure data consistency, scalability, and fault tolerance across your systems.

Utilizing Event-Driven Architecture: Leveraging Triggers and Streams for Real-Time Data Synchronization

Event-driven architecture (EDA) is a powerful approach for building scalable and responsive applications. It involves producing, detecting, consuming, and reacting to events in real time. By leveraging triggers and streams, EDA can synchronize data across different systems, ensuring consistency and enabling real-time updates. This guide focuses on using EDA for real-time data synchronization between PostgreSQL and DynamoDB while building RESTful APIs.

Understanding Event-Driven Architecture

Event-driven architecture revolves around events, which are significant changes or occurrences within a system. An event can be anything from a user action (e.g., a new user registration) to a system state change (e.g., an updated database record).

Key components of EDA include:

- **Event Producers:** Components that generate events.

- **Event Consumers:** Components that listen for and process events.

- **Event Channels:** Mechanisms (e.g., message queues, streams) that transport events from producers to consumers.

- **Event Processors:** Services or functions that handle and act on events.

Benefits of Event-Driven Architecture

EDA offers several benefits:

- **Scalability**: Decouples components, allowing them to scale independently.

- **Responsiveness**: Enables real-time reactions to events.

- **Flexibility**: Facilitates adding or modifying components without impacting the entire system.

- **Resilience**: Isolates failures to specific components, enhancing fault tolerance.

Leveraging Triggers and Streams for Real-Time Data Synchronization

To illustrate the use of EDA for real time data synchronization, we'll build an example where changes in a PostgreSQL database are reflected in a DynamoDB table using triggers and streams.

Step 1: Setting Up PostgreSQL Triggers

Triggers in PostgreSQL are special procedures that are automatically executed in response to specific database operations (e.g., `INSERT`, `UPDATE`, `DELETE`).

Creating a PostgreSQL Table

First, create a PostgreSQL table to manage user data:

```sql
CREATE TABLE users (
  user_id SERIAL PRIMARY KEY,
  username VARCHAR(50) UNIQUE NOT NULL,
  email VARCHAR(100) UNIQUE NOT NULL,
  created_at TIMESTAMP DEFAULT CURRENT_TIMESTAMP
);
```

Adding a Trigger Function

Next, create a trigger function that will capture changes and send notifications to a channel.

```sql
CREATE OR REPLACE FUNCTION notify_dynamodb() RETURNS TRIGGER AS $$
DECLARE
  record JSON;
BEGIN
  record = row_to_json(NEW);
  PERFORM pg_notify('dynamodb_channel', record::text);
```

```
  RETURN NEW;
END;
$$ LANGUAGE plpgsql;
```

Adding a Trigger

Create a trigger to call the function after an `INSERT` operation on the `users` table:

```sql
CREATE TRIGGER user_insert
AFTER INSERT ON users
FOR EACH ROW EXECUTE FUNCTION
notify_dynamodb();
```

Step 2: Setting Up a Listener for PostgreSQL Notifications

We need a listener to handle the notifications sent to the `dynamodb_channel` and update DynamoDB accordingly.

Listener Implementation with Node.js

We'll use Node.js to listen to PostgreSQL notifications and update DynamoDB.

Step 2.1: Setting Up the Environment

Install the required packages:

```bash
npm install pg aws-sdk
```

Step 2.2: Writing the Listener Script

Create a script (`listener.js`) that listens for notifications and updates DynamoDB:

```javascript
const { Client } = require('pg');
const AWS = require('aws-sdk');

const dynamoDB = new AWS.DynamoDB.DocumentClient();
const client = new Client({
  user: 'postgres',
  host: 'localhost',
  database: 'mydb',
  password: 'password',
  port: 5432,
});
```

```
client.connect();
client.query('LISTEN dynamodb_channel');

client.on('notification', async (msg) => {
  const data = JSON.parse(msg.payload);
  const params = {
    TableName: 'UsersTable',
    Item: {
      user_id: data.user_id,
      username: data.username,
      email: data.email,
      created_at: data.created_at,
  };
  try {
    await dynamoDB.put(params).promise();
    console.log('Data synced to DynamoDB:', data);
  } catch (error) {
    console.error('Error syncing data to DynamoDB:', error);
});

console.log('Listening for notifications...');
```

Step 3: Setting Up DynamoDB

Create a DynamoDB table to store user data:

```javascript
const AWS = require('aws-sdk');
const dynamoDB = new AWS.DynamoDB({ region: 'us-east-1' });

const createTableParams = {
  TableName: 'UsersTable',
  KeySchema: [
    { AttributeName: 'user_id', KeyType: 'HASH' }, // Partition key
  ],
  AttributeDefinitions: [
    { AttributeName: 'user_id', AttributeType: 'N' },
  ],
  ProvisionedThroughput: {
    ReadCapacityUnits: 5,
    WriteCapacityUnits: 5,
};

dynamoDB.createTable(createTableParams, (err, data) => {
  if (err) {
    console.error('Error creating DynamoDB table:', JSON.stringify(err, null, 2));
  } else {
    console.log('DynamoDB table created successfully:', JSON.stringify(data, null, 2));
});
```

```

## Step 4: Building RESTful APIs

With the event-driven components in place, we can now build RESTful API endpoints using Express.js.

### Setting Up Express.js

Install Express.js:

```bash
npm install express body-parser
```

Implementing the API Endpoints

Create an API server (`server.js`) that provides endpoints for user management:

```javascript
const express = require('express');
const bodyParser = require('body-parser');
const { Pool } = require('pg');
const AWS = require('aws-sdk');

const app = express();
const pool = new Pool({

```javascript
  user: 'postgres',
  host: 'localhost',
  database: 'mydb',
  password: 'password',
  port: 5432,
});

const dynamoDB = new AWS.DynamoDB.DocumentClient();

app.use(bodyParser.json());

// Endpoint to create a new user
app.post('/users', async (req, res) => {
  const { username, email } = req.body;
  try {
    const result = await pool.query('INSERT INTO users (username, email) VALUES ($1, $2) RETURNING *', [username, email]);
    res.json(result.rows[0]);
  } catch (error) {
    console.error('Error creating user:', error);
    res.status(500).json({ error: 'An error occurred while creating the user.' });
  }
});

// Endpoint to fetch user details
app.get('/users/:user_id', async (req, res) => {
```

```javascript
  const { user_id } = req.params;
  try {
    const result = await pool.query('SELECT * FROM users WHERE user_id = $1', [user_id]);
    if (result.rows.length > 0) {
      res.json(result.rows[0]);
    } else {
      res.status(404).json({ message: 'User not found.' });
    }
  } catch (error) {
    console.error('Error fetching user details:', error)
    res.status(500).json({ error: 'An error occurred while fetching user details.' });
  }
});

// Endpoint to fetch user activities from DynamoDB
app.get('/users/:user_id/activity', async (req, res) => {
  const { user_id } = req.params;

  const params = {
    TableName: 'UsersTable',
    KeyConditionExpression: 'user_id = :user_id',
    ExpressionAttributeValues: {
      ':user_id': parseInt(user_id)
    }
  };

  try {
```

```
    const data = await
dynamoDB.query(params).promise();
    res.json(data.Items);
  } catch (error) {
    console.error('Error fetching user activities:', error);
    res.status(500).json({ error: 'An error occurred while fetching user activities.' });
});

const PORT = process.env.PORT || 3000;
app.listen(PORT, () => {
  console.log(`Server is running on port ${PORT}`);
});
```

Testing the Setup

To test the integration, follow these steps:

1. Start the PostgreSQL Listener:

```bash
node listener.js
```

This script listens for notifications from PostgreSQL and updates DynamoDB.

2. Run the Express.js Server:

```bash
node server.js
```

This script starts the RESTful API server.

3. Create a New User: Send a POST request to the `/users` endpoint to create a new user.

```bash
curl -X POST http://localhost:3000/users -H "Content-Type: application/json" -d '{"username": "john_doe", "email": "john@example.com"}'
```

This action triggers the PostgreSQL trigger, which sends a notification to the listener. The listener then updates DynamoDB with the new user data.

4. Fetch User Details: Send a GET request to the `/users/:user_id` endpoint to fetch user details from PostgreSQL.

```bash
curl http://localhost:3000/users/1
```

5. Fetch User Activities: Send a GET request to the `/users/:user_id/activity` endpoint to fetch user activities from DynamoDB.

```bash
curl http://localhost:3000/users/1/activity
```

Extending the Architecture

This basic setup can be extended in various ways to handle more complex scenarios and improve robustness.

Handling Updates and Deletes

To handle updates and deletes, you can create additional triggers and functions in PostgreSQL:

```sql
-- Trigger function for updates
CREATE OR REPLACE FUNCTION notify_dynamodb_update() RETURNS TRIGGER AS $$
DECLARE
  record JSON;
BEGIN
  record = row_to_json(NEW);
```

```sql
    PERFORM pg_notify('dynamodb_update_channel', record::text);
    RETURN NEW;
END;
$$ LANGUAGE plpgsql;

-- Trigger for updates
CREATE TRIGGER user_update
AFTER UPDATE ON users
FOR EACH ROW EXECUTE FUNCTION notify_dynamodb_update();

-- Trigger function for deletes
CREATE OR REPLACE FUNCTION notify_dynamodb_delete() RETURNS TRIGGER AS $$
DECLARE
    record JSON;
BEGIN
    record = row_to_json(OLD);
    PERFORM pg_notify('dynamodb_delete_channel', record::text);
    RETURN OLD;
END;
$$ LANGUAGE plpgsql;

-- Trigger for deletes
CREATE TRIGGER user_delete
AFTER DELETE ON users
```

```
FOR EACH ROW EXECUTE FUNCTION
notify_dynamodb_delete();
```

Then, update your Node.js listener to handle these new events:

```javascript
client.query('LISTEN dynamodb_update_channel');
client.query('LISTEN dynamodb_delete_channel');

client.on('notification', async (msg) => {
  const data = JSON.parse(msg.payload);

  if (msg.channel === 'dynamodb_channel') {
   const params = {
     TableName: 'UsersTable',
     Item: {
       user_id: data.user_id,
       username: data.username,
       email: data.email,
       created_at: data.created_at,
     },
   };
   try {
     await dynamoDB.put(params).promise();
     console.log('Data synced to DynamoDB:', data);
   } catch (error) {
```

```
      console.error('Error syncing data to DynamoDB:',
error);
    }
  } else if (msg.channel ===
'dynamodb_update_channel') {
    const params = {
      TableName: 'UsersTable',
      Item: {
        user_id: data.user_id,
        username: data.username,
        email: data.email,
        created_at: data.created_at,
    };
    try {
      await dynamoDB.put(params).promise();
      console.log('Data updated in DynamoDB:', data);
    } catch (error) {
      console.error('Error updating data in DynamoDB:',
error);
    }
  } else if (msg.channel === 'dynamodb_delete_channel')
{
    const params = {
      TableName: 'UsersTable',
      Key: {
        user_id: data.user_id,
    };
    try {
```

```
    await dynamoDB.delete(params).promise();
    console.log('Data deleted from DynamoDB:', data);
  } catch (error) {
    console.error('Error deleting data from DynamoDB:', error);
  }
});
```

Monitoring and Error Handling

To ensure the robustness of your system, implement monitoring and error handling:

- **Retry Logic:** Implement retry logic for failed DynamoDB operations.

- **Logging**: Use a logging library to track errors and operations.

- **Alerts**: Set up alerts to notify you of critical failures.

Leveraging event-driven architecture with triggers and streams is a powerful approach for real-time data synchronization. By combining PostgreSQL triggers with DynamoDB streams and a robust RESTful API, you can ensure data consistency and responsiveness in your applications. This architecture scales well and provides flexibility, allowing you to adapt to changing requirements and expanding functionalities. Whether you're building a simple application or a complex system, EDA offers the tools and patterns needed to create efficient, scalable, and resilient data synchronization solutions.

Building a Hybrid Data Model: Mapping Data Between DynamoDB and PostgreSQL Effectively

In today's data-driven world, leveraging multiple databases to store and manage data is a common practice. Using both relational databases like PostgreSQL and NoSQL databases like DynamoDB allows you to harness the strengths of each system to optimize performance, scalability, and flexibility. However, this approach introduces complexity in terms of data modeling, consistency, and integration. This article will guide you through the process of building a hybrid data model, effectively mapping data between DynamoDB and PostgreSQL, and integrating these databases into a cohesive system using RESTful APIs.

Why Use a Hybrid Data Model?

PostgreSQL is a powerful, open-source relational database system known for its robustness, ACID compliance, and rich feature set, including complex queries, transactions, and joins.

DynamoDB, managed by AWS, is a scalable NoSQL database that offers high availability and low latency, making it ideal for applications requiring fast and reliable access to non-relational data.

By combining these databases, you can achieve:

- **Scalability**: Handle high-velocity data with DynamoDB while managing relational data with PostgreSQL.

- **Performance**: Optimize read and write operations using the strengths of each database.

- **Flexibility**: Utilize PostgreSQL for complex queries and transactions, and DynamoDB for fast, scalable access.

Designing the Hybrid Data Model

When designing a hybrid data model, it is essential to define clear boundaries and responsibilities for each database. Here are some considerations:

1. Data Types: Determine which data types and structures are best suited for each database.

2. Access Patterns: Identify the access patterns and query requirements for your data.

3. Consistency: Ensure data consistency across databases, especially for operations that span both systems.

Example Use Case: User Management and Activity Logging

For this example, we will manage user information in PostgreSQL and log user activities in DynamoDB.

- **User Management:** Store user details (e.g., username, email) in PostgreSQL.

- **Activity Logging:** Store user activity logs (e.g., login events) in DynamoDB.

Step 1: Setting Up PostgreSQL

First, set up the PostgreSQL database to store user information.

<u>Creating the PostgreSQL Table</u>

```sql
CREATE TABLE users (
  user_id SERIAL PRIMARY KEY,
  username VARCHAR(50) UNIQUE NOT NULL,
  email VARCHAR(100) UNIQUE NOT NULL,
  created_at TIMESTAMP DEFAULT CURRENT_TIMESTAMP
);
```

Step 2: Setting Up DynamoDB

Next, set up the DynamoDB table to log user activities.

Creating the DynamoDB Table

```javascript
const AWS = require('aws-sdk');
const dynamoDB = new AWS.DynamoDB({ region: 'us-east-1' });

const createTableParams = {
  TableName: 'UserActivities',
  KeySchema: [
    { AttributeName: 'user_id', KeyType: 'HASH' }, // Partition key
```

```
    { AttributeName: 'activity_id', KeyType: 'RANGE' }
// Sort key
  ],
  AttributeDefinitions: [
    { AttributeName: 'user_id', AttributeType: 'N' },
    { AttributeName: 'activity_id', AttributeType: 'S' }
  ],
  ProvisionedThroughput: {
    ReadCapacityUnits: 5,
    WriteCapacityUnits: 5
};

dynamoDB.createTable(createTableParams, (err, data) => {
  if (err) {
    console.error('Error creating DynamoDB table:',
JSON.stringify(err, null, 2));
  } else {
    console.log('DynamoDB table created successfully:',
JSON.stringify(data, null, 2));
  }
});
```

Step 3: Building RESTful APIs

We will build RESTful API endpoints using Express.js to handle user management and activity logging.

Setting Up Express.js

Install the necessary packages:

```bash
npm install express body-parser pg aws-sdk
```

Implementing the API Server

Create an API server (`server.js`) to handle the operations:

```javascript
const express = require('express');
const bodyParser = require('body-parser');
const { Pool } = require('pg');
const AWS = require('aws-sdk');
const { v4: uuidv4 } = require('uuid');

const app = express();
const pool = new Pool({
  user: 'postgres',
  host: 'localhost',
  database: 'mydb',
  password: 'password',
  port: 5432,
});
```

```javascript
const dynamoDB = new AWS.DynamoDB.DocumentClient();

app.use(bodyParser.json());

// Endpoint to create a new user
app.post('/users', async (req, res) => {
  const { username, email } = req.body;
  try {
    const result = await pool.query('INSERT INTO users (username, email) VALUES ($1, $2) RETURNING *', [username, email]);
    res.json(result.rows[0]);
  } catch (error) {
    console.error('Error creating user:', error);
    res.status(500).json({ error: 'An error occurred while creating the user.' });
  }
});

// Endpoint to log user activity
app.post('/users/:user_id/activity', async (req, res) => {
  const { user_id } = req.params;
  const { activity_type, description } = req.body;
  const activity_id = uuidv4();

  const params = {
    TableName: 'UserActivities',
```

```
    Item: {
      user_id: parseInt(user_id),
      activity_id,
      activity_type,
      description,
      timestamp: new Date().toISOString()
  };

  try {
    await dynamoDB.put(params).promise();
    res.status(201).json({ message: 'Activity logged
successfully.' });
  } catch (error) {
    console.error('Error logging activity:', error);
    res.status(500).json({ error: 'An error occurred while
logging the activity.' });
  }
});

// Endpoint to fetch user details from PostgreSQL
app.get('/users/:user_id', async (req, res) => {
  const { user_id } = req.params;
  try {
    const result = await pool.query('SELECT * FROM
users WHERE user_id = $1', [user_id]);
    if (result.rows.length > 0) {
      res.json(result.rows[0]);
    } else {
      res.status(404).json({ message: 'User not found.' });
```

```
    }
  } catch (error) {
    console.error('Error fetching user details:', error);
    res.status(500).json({ error: 'An error occurred while fetching user details.' });
});

// Endpoint to fetch user activities from DynamoDB
app.get('/users/:user_id/activity', async (req, res) => {
  const { user_id } = req.params;

  const params = {
    TableName: 'UserActivities',
    KeyConditionExpression: 'user_id = :user_id',
    ExpressionAttributeValues: {
      ':user_id': parseInt(user_id)
    }
  };

  try {
    const data = await dynamoDB.query(params).promise();
    res.json(data.Items);
  } catch (error) {
    console.error('Error fetching user activities:', error);
    res.status(500).json({ error: 'An error occurred while fetching user activities.' });
});
```

```javascript
const PORT = process.env.PORT || 3000;
app.listen(PORT, () => {
  console.log(`Server is running on port ${PORT}`);
});
```

Step 4: Ensuring Data Consistency

Ensuring data consistency across PostgreSQL and DynamoDB is critical. Here are strategies to maintain consistency:

Using Transactions in PostgreSQL

PostgreSQL supports transactions to ensure atomic operations. You can use transactions when making changes to the database to ensure consistency:

```javascript
app.post('/users', async (req, res) => {
  const { username, email } = req.body;
  const client = await pool.connect();
  try {
    await client.query('BEGIN');
    const result = await client.query('INSERT INTO users (username, email) VALUES ($1, $2) RETURNING *', [username, email]);
    await client.query('COMMIT');
```

```
    res.json(result.rows[0]);
  } catch (error) {
    await client.query('ROLLBACK');
    console.error('Error creating user:', error);
    res.status(500).json({ error: 'An error occurred while creating the user.' });
  } finally {
    client.release();
  }
});
```

Implementing Event-Driven Updates

For cross-database consistency, an event-driven approach can help. You can use AWS SNS (Simple Notification Service) to notify the application of changes that should be reflected in both databases.

Step 4.1: Setting Up AWS SNS

Create an SNS topic to handle user updates:

```javascript
const AWS = require('aws-sdk');
const sns = new AWS.SNS({ region: 'us-east-1' });

sns.createTopic({ Name: 'UserUpdates' }, (err, data) =>
{
```

```
if (err) {
  console.error('Error creating SNS topic:', err);
} else {
  console.log('SNS topic created successfully:', data.TopicArn);
}
});
```

Step 4.2: Publishing Events

Modify the user creation endpoint to publish an event to the SNS topic:

```javascript
const { Pool } = require('pg');
const AWS = require('aws-sdk');
const sns = new AWS.SNS({ region: 'us-east-1' });
const pool = new Pool({ /* PostgreSQL connection parameters */ });

app.post('/users', async (req, res) => {
  const { username, email } = req.body;
  const client = await pool.connect();
  try {
    await client.query('BEGIN');
    const result = await client.query('INSERT INTO users (username, email) VALUES ($1, $2) RETURNING *', [username, email]);
```

```
    const user = result.rows[0];

    // Publish an event to SNS
    const params = {
      Message: JSON.stringify({
        user_id: user.user_id,
        username: user.username,
        email: user.email,
        event: 'USER_CREATED'
      }),
      TopicArn: 'arn:aws:sns:us-east-1:123456789012:UserUpdates'
    };
    await sns.publish(params).promise();

    await client.query('COMMIT');
    res.json(user);
  } catch (error) {
    await client.query('ROLLBACK');
    console.error('Error creating user:', error);
    res.status(500).json({ error: 'An error occurred while creating the user.' });
  } finally {
    client.release();
  }
});
```

Step 4.3: Subscribing to the SNS Topic

Create an AWS Lambda function to subscribe to the SNS topic and handle updates:

Lambda Function Handler (`index.js`):

```javascript
const AWS = require('aws-sdk');
const dynamoDB = new AWS.DynamoDB.DocumentClient();
const pool = new Pool({
  user: 'postgres',
  host: 'localhost',
  database: 'mydb',
  password: 'password',
  port: 5432,
});

exports.handler = async (event) => {
  for (const record of event.Records) {
    const message = JSON.parse(record.Sns.Message);

    if (message.event === 'USER_CREATED') {
      const { user_id, username, email } = message;

      // Insert into DynamoDB
      const params = {
        TableName: 'UserActivities',
```

```javascript
    Item: {
      user_id: user_id,
      activity_id: uuidv4(),
      activity_type: 'USER_CREATED',
      description: `User ${username} created with email ${email}`,
      timestamp: new Date().toISOString()
    };

    try {
      await dynamoDB.put(params).promise();
      console.log('User activity logged in DynamoDB:', params.Item);
    } catch (error) {
      console.error('Error logging user activity in DynamoDB:', error);
    }
};
```

Deploy the Lambda function and create a subscription to the SNS topic:

Create Subscription:

```javascript
const params = {
  Protocol: 'lambda',
```

```
  TopicArn: 'arn:aws:sns:us-east-
1:123456789012:UserUpdates',
  Endpoint: 'arn:aws:lambda:us-east-
1:123456789012:function:YourLambdaFunctionName'
};

sns.subscribe(params, (err, data) => {
  if (err) {
    console.error('Error creating SNS subscription:', err);
  } else {
    console.log('SNS subscription created successfully:', data.SubscriptionArn);
  }
});
```

Step 5: Querying Data from Both Databases

To fetch data that spans both databases, you can create composite API endpoints that retrieve data from PostgreSQL and DynamoDB and combine the results.

Composite Endpoint to Fetch User and Activities:

```javascript
app.get('/users/:user_id/full', async (req, res) => {
  const { user_id } = req.params;

  try {
```

```javascript
    // Fetch user details from PostgreSQL
    const userResult = await pool.query('SELECT * FROM users WHERE user_id = $1', [user_id]);
    if (userResult.rows.length === 0) {
      return res.status(404).json({ message: 'User not found.' });
    }
    const user = userResult.rows[0];

    // Fetch user activities from DynamoDB
    const activityParams = {
      TableName: 'UserActivities',
      KeyConditionExpression: 'user_id = :user_id',
      ExpressionAttributeValues: {
        ':user_id': parseInt(user_id)
      }
    };

    const activityResult = await dynamoDB.query(activityParams).promise();
    const activities = activityResult.Items;

    // Combine and return the result
    res.json({ user, activities });
  } catch (error) {
    console.error('Error fetching user data:', error);
    res.status(500).json({ error: 'An error occurred while fetching user data.' });
  }
});
```

Building a hybrid data model that maps data effectively between DynamoDB and PostgreSQL involves careful planning, design, and implementation. By leveraging the strengths of both databases, you can achieve scalability, performance, and flexibility while maintaining data consistency.

Key Takeaways:

- **Data Modeling:** Define clear boundaries for data storage based on the strengths of each database.

- **Consistency**: Ensure data consistency across databases using transactions, event-driven updates, and robust error handling.

- **Integration**: Build RESTful APIs to provide seamless access to data stored in different databases.

With these strategies, you can create a powerful and efficient hybrid data model that meets the needs of modern applications. This approach not only optimizes performance and scalability but also enhances the overall architecture, making it more resilient and adaptable to future changes.

Best Practices for Integration: Optimizing Performance, Reliability, and Scalability

Integrating RESTful APIs with databases like DynamoDB and PostgreSQL is essential for building robust, scalable, and high-performance applications. This guide provides best practices for optimizing performance, reliability, and scalability when building RESTful APIs with DynamoDB and PostgreSQL. We will cover architectural decisions, coding practices, and strategies for database management, illustrated with code examples.

Architectural Decisions

1. Choosing the Right Database

DynamoDB

Amazon DynamoDB is a fully managed NoSQL database known for its high performance, scalability, and low latency. It is ideal for applications that require seamless scalability and can handle high-velocity data with variable schema.

PostgreSQL

PostgreSQL is a powerful, open-source relational database system. It is well-suited for applications requiring complex queries, transactional integrity, and adherence to ACID properties.

2. Hybrid Architecture

A hybrid architecture leveraging both DynamoDB and PostgreSQL can be beneficial. For instance, DynamoDB can handle high-velocity, unstructured data, while PostgreSQL can manage structured data requiring complex queries and transactions.

3. API Design

RESTful APIs should follow the principles of Representational State Transfer (REST), using standard HTTP methods and status codes, and ensuring stateless operations.

Coding Practices

1. Efficient Data Modeling

DynamoDB

In DynamoDB, design tables to accommodate access patterns. Use partition keys and sort keys effectively to minimize hot partitions and evenly distribute data across nodes.

```python
import boto3

# Initialize DynamoDB resource
dynamodb = boto3.resource('dynamodb')

# Create a DynamoDB table
table = dynamodb.create_table(
    TableName='Users',
    KeySchema=[
        {
            'AttributeName': 'UserID',
            'KeyType': 'HASH'  # Partition key
        },
            'AttributeName': 'Timestamp',
            'KeyType': 'RANGE'  # Sort key
        }
    AttributeDefinitions=[
        {
            'AttributeName': 'UserID',
            'AttributeType': 'S'
        },
            'AttributeName': 'Timestamp',
            'AttributeType': 'N'
        }
```

```
    ProvisionedThroughput={
        'ReadCapacityUnits': 5,
        'WriteCapacityUnits': 5
    }
```

PostgreSQL

Normalize the database schema to reduce redundancy and improve data integrity. Use appropriate indexing to speed up query performance.

```sql
CREATE TABLE Users (
    UserID SERIAL PRIMARY KEY,
    Username VARCHAR(50) UNIQUE NOT NULL,
    Email VARCHAR(50) UNIQUE NOT NULL,
    CreatedAt TIMESTAMP DEFAULT CURRENT_TIMESTAMP
);

CREATE INDEX idx_username ON Users (Username);
CREATE INDEX idx_email ON Users (Email);
```

2. Efficient Querying

DynamoDB

Use Query and Scan operations appropriately. Prefer Query over Scan to avoid full table scans.

```python
# Querying DynamoDB table
response = table.query(
    KeyConditionExpression=Key('UserID').eq('12345')
    & Key('Timestamp').between(1610000000,
1620000000)
)
items = response['Items']
```

PostgreSQL

Write efficient SQL queries and use prepared statements to prevent SQL injection and improve performance.

```python
import psycopg2

# Connect to PostgreSQL
conn = psycopg2.connect("dbname=test user=postgres password=secret")
cur = conn.cursor()

# Use prepared statements
```

```
cur.execute("PREPARE user_query AS SELECT *
FROM Users WHERE UserID = $1;")
cur.execute("EXECUTE user_query (%s);", (12345,))
user = cur.fetchone()

cur.close()
conn.close()
```

3. Caching

Implement caching mechanisms to reduce database load and improve response times. Use in-memory caches like Redis or Memcached.

```python
import redis

# Initialize Redis client
redis_client = redis.StrictRedis(host='localhost', port=6379, db=0)

# Caching a query result
user_id = 12345
user = redis_client.get(f"user:{user_id}")
if not user:
    # Fetch from PostgreSQL or DynamoDB
    user = fetch_user_from_db(user_id)
```

```
redis_client.set(f"user:{user_id}", user, ex=300)  #
Cache for 5 minutes
```
```

## Database Management Strategies

### 1. Backup and Recovery

Regularly backup your databases and have a recovery plan in place. Use automated backup services provided by AWS for DynamoDB and PostgreSQL.

### DynamoDB

Enable point-in-time recovery (PITR) and create on-demand backups.

```python
# Enable point-in-time recovery
dynamodb.update_continuous_backups(
    TableName='Users',
    PointInTimeRecoverySpecification={
        'PointInTimeRecoveryEnabled': True
    }
```
```

PostgreSQL

Schedule regular backups using pg_dump or use managed services like AWS RDS.

```bash
# Using pg_dump for backup
pg_dump -U postgres -F c -b -v -f /path/to/backup/backup_file.sql dbname
```

2. Monitoring and Alerts

Set up monitoring and alerts to detect and respond to issues promptly. Use Amazon CloudWatch for DynamoDB and PostgreSQL.

DynamoDB

Monitor key metrics like read/write capacity, throttled requests, and latency.

```python
# CloudWatch example for monitoring DynamoDB
cloudwatch = boto3.client('cloudwatch')

# Create an alarm for high read capacity usage
cloudwatch.put_metric_alarm(
    AlarmName='HighReadCapacity',
    MetricName='ConsumedReadCapacityUnits',
```

```
        Namespace='AWS/DynamoDB',
        Statistic='Sum',
        Period=300,
        EvaluationPeriods=1,
        Threshold=1000,

ComparisonOperator='GreaterThanOrEqualToThreshold
',
        Dimensions=[
            {
                'Name': 'TableName',
                'Value': 'Users'
            }        AlarmActions=['arn:aws:sns:us-east-1:123456789012:NotifyMe']
)
```

PostgreSQL

Monitor metrics such as CPU usage, connection count, and query performance. Use tools like pgAdmin or AWS RDS Performance Insights.

```sql
-- Query to check for long-running queries
SELECT pid, age(clock_timestamp(), query_start),
usename, query
FROM pg_stat_activity
```

```
WHERE state != 'idle' AND now() - query_start >
interval '5 minutes';
```

3. Scaling

DynamoDB

DynamoDB offers on-demand scaling. Adjust read and write capacity units based on usage patterns.

```python
# Update table to use on-demand capacity mode
dynamodb.update_table(
    TableName='Users',
    BillingMode='PAY_PER_REQUEST'
)
```

PostgreSQL

Use connection pooling to manage database connections efficiently. Scale vertically by increasing instance size or horizontally by partitioning the database.

```python
# Example of using connection pooling with Psycopg2
from psycopg2 import pool
```

```
# Initialize connection pool
pg_pool = pool.SimpleConnectionPool(1, 20,
user="postgres", password="secret", host="localhost",
port="5432", database="test")

# Get a connection from the pool
conn = pg_pool.getconn()
cur = conn.cursor()
cur.execute("SELECT * FROM Users;")
users = cur.fetchall()
cur.close()
pg_pool.putconn(conn)
```
```

## Reliability and High Availability

### 1. Multi-AZ Deployments

Deploy databases across multiple Availability Zones (AZs) to ensure high availability and fault tolerance.

### DynamoDB

DynamoDB automatically replicates data across multiple AZs, providing built-in high availability.

### PostgreSQL
```

Use Amazon RDS for PostgreSQL with Multi-AZ deployments to ensure automatic failover in case of an outage.

```python
# AWS CLI command to create an RDS instance with Multi-AZ
aws rds create-db-instance \
    --db-instance-identifier mydbinstance \
    --db-instance-class db.t3.medium \
    --engine postgres \
    --allocated-storage 20 \
    --master-username masteruser \
    --master-user-password masterpassword \
    --multi-az
```

2. Read Replicas

Use read replicas to offload read traffic and enhance performance.

DynamoDB

DynamoDB global tables provide a fully replicated, multi-region setup.

```python
# Creating a global table in DynamoDB
dynamodb.create_global_table(
    GlobalTableName='Users',
    ReplicationGroup=[
        {
            'RegionName': 'us-east-1'
        },
            'RegionName': 'eu-west-1'
        }
```

PostgreSQL

Set up read replicas for PostgreSQL to distribute read queries and reduce load on the primary database.

```python
# AWS CLI command to create a read replica in RDS
aws rds create-db-instance-read-replica \
    --db-instance-identifier mydbreadreplica \
    --source-db-instance-identifier mydbinstance \
    --db-instance-class db.t3.medium
```

Security Practices

1. Encryption

Encrypt data at rest and in transit to protect sensitive information.

DynamoDB

Enable encryption at rest using AWS Key Management Service (KMS).

```python
# Enable encryption at rest for DynamoDB table
dynamodb.create_table(
    TableName='Users',
    ...
    SSESpecification={
        'Enabled': True,
        'SSEType': 'KMS',
        'KMSMasterKeyId': 'alias/aws/dynamodb'
    }
```

PostgreSQL

Use SSL/TLS for encrypting data in transit and enable disk encryption for data at rest.

```sql
```

```
-- Enable SSL in PostgreSQL configuration (postgresql.conf)
# PostgreSQL SSL Configuration (postgresql.conf)
ssl = on
ssl_cert_file = '/path/to/server.crt'
ssl_key_file = '/path/to/server.key'
```

2. Access Control

Implement strict access control measures to ensure only authorized users can access the database.

DynamoDB

Use AWS Identity and Access Management (IAM) roles and policies to control access to DynamoDB tables.

```json
{
  "Version": "2012-10-17",
  "Statement": [
    {
      "Effect": "Allow",
      "Action": [
        "dynamodb:PutItem",
        "dynamodb:GetItem",
        "dynamodb:UpdateItem",
```

```
        "dynamodb:DeleteItem"
    ],
    "Resource": "arn:aws:dynamodb:us-east-1:123456789012:table/Users"
}
```

PostgreSQL

Create roles with specific privileges and use role-based access control (RBAC) to manage permissions.

```sql
-- Create a read-only role in PostgreSQL
CREATE ROLE readonly;
GRANT CONNECT ON DATABASE test TO readonly;
GRANT USAGE ON SCHEMA public TO readonly;
GRANT SELECT ON ALL TABLES IN SCHEMA public TO readonly;
ALTER DEFAULT PRIVILEGES IN SCHEMA public GRANT SELECT ON TABLES TO readonly;

-- Assign role to a user
CREATE USER readonly_user WITH PASSWORD 'readonly_password';
GRANT readonly TO readonly_user;
```

3. Auditing and Logging

Enable logging and auditing to track database activities and detect suspicious behaviors.

DynamoDB

Use AWS CloudTrail to log DynamoDB API calls for auditing purposes.

```python
# Enabling CloudTrail for DynamoDB
cloudtrail = boto3.client('cloudtrail')

cloudtrail.create_trail(
    Name='DynamoDBTrail',
    S3BucketName='my-cloudtrail-bucket',
    IncludeGlobalServiceEvents=True,
    IsMultiRegionTrail=True,
    EnableLogFileValidation=True
)
```

PostgreSQL

Enable logging in PostgreSQL to track query execution and access patterns.

```sql
# PostgreSQL logging configuration (postgresql.conf)
logging_collector = on
log_directory = 'log'
log_filename = 'postgresql-%a.log'
log_statement = 'all'
log_duration = on
```

API Design Patterns

1. Pagination

Implement pagination to handle large datasets efficiently.

```python
# DynamoDB pagination example
def scan_table(table, limit=10, last_evaluated_key=None):
    params = {
        'TableName': table,
        'Limit': limit
    }
    if last_evaluated_key:
        params['ExclusiveStartKey'] = last_evaluated_key

    response = dynamodb.scan(**params)
```

```
    items = response['Items']
    last_evaluated_key = response.get('LastEvaluatedKey', None)

    return items, last_evaluated_key
```

```python
# PostgreSQL pagination example
def get_paginated_users(offset=0, limit=10):
    query = "SELECT * FROM Users ORDER BY CreatedAt DESC LIMIT %s OFFSET %s;"
    cur.execute(query, (limit, offset))
    return cur.fetchall()
```

2. Rate Limiting

Implement rate limiting to protect your API from abuse and ensure fair usage.

```python
from flask_limiter import Limiter
from flask_limiter.util import get_remote_address
from flask import Flask

app = Flask(__name__)
limiter = Limiter(
```

```
    app,
    key_func=get_remote_address,
    default_limits=["200 per day", "50 per hour"]
)

@app.route("/resource")
@limiter.limit("10 per minute")
def limited_resource():
    return "This is a rate limited resource."
```

3. Idempotency

Ensure that API operations are idempotent, particularly for write operations, to avoid unintended consequences from repeated requests.

```python
from flask import Flask, request, jsonify
import hashlib

app = Flask(__name__)
requests_cache = {}

@app.route("/process", methods=["POST"])
def process_request():
    request_id = hashlib.sha256(request.data).hexdigest()
```

```
    if request_id in requests_cache:
        return jsonify({"status": "duplicate"}), 409

    # Process the request
    requests_cache[request_id] = True
    # Perform your processing logic here
    return jsonify({"status": "processed"})
```

Building RESTful APIs with DynamoDB and PostgreSQL involves several best practices to optimize performance, reliability, and scalability. By carefully choosing the right database for each use case, efficiently modeling data, implementing effective querying techniques, and incorporating caching strategies, you can enhance the performance of your API. Ensuring robust database management with regular backups, monitoring, and appropriate scaling measures will improve reliability. Implementing security practices such as encryption, access control, and logging will safeguard your data. Following these best practices will help you build a resilient, high-performance API that can scale with your application's demands.

Chapter 6

Designing the Data Model: Separating User Profiles (PostgreSQL) and Real-Time Activity (DynamoDB)

In modern application development, it's crucial to choose the right databases for the right type of data. This often involves a hybrid approach where different databases are used to optimize performance, scalability, and flexibility. In this article, we will design a data model that separates user profiles into PostgreSQL and real-time activity into DynamoDB. Additionally, we'll build a RESTful API that interacts with these databases.

Why Separate User Profiles and Real-Time Activity?

User Profiles: User profiles typically contain structured, relational data that is often queried and updated in transactions. This includes user information such as names, email addresses, preferences, and other metadata. PostgreSQL is an ideal choice for this type of data due to its ACID compliance, complex querying capabilities, and robust indexing.

Real-Time Activity: Real-time activity data involves high-velocity, high-volume writes and reads, such as user interactions, clicks, page views, and other events.

This data is often used for analytics, monitoring, and real-time decision making. DynamoDB, with its scalable and low-latency performance, is well-suited for such use cases.

Designing the Data Model

PostgreSQL Schema for User Profiles:

1. Users Table:

- `id`: Primary Key (UUID)
- `username`: Unique Username
- `email`: Unique Email
- `created_at`: Timestamp of Account Creation
- `updated_at`: Timestamp of Last Update

2. Profiles Table:

- `id`: Primary Key (UUID)
- `user_id`: Foreign Key to Users Table
- `first_name`: First Name

- `last_name`: Last Name

- `date_of_birth`: Date of Birth

- `bio`: User Bio

```sql
CREATE TABLE users (
  id UUID PRIMARY KEY DEFAULT gen_random_uuid(),
  username VARCHAR(50) UNIQUE NOT NULL,
  email VARCHAR(100) UNIQUE NOT NULL,
  created_at TIMESTAMPTZ DEFAULT NOW(),
  updated_at TIMESTAMPTZ DEFAULT NOW()
);

CREATE TABLE profiles (
  id UUID PRIMARY KEY DEFAULT gen_random_uuid(),
  user_id UUID REFERENCES users(id) ON DELETE CASCADE,
  first_name VARCHAR(50),
  last_name VARCHAR(50),
  date_of_birth DATE,
  bio TEXT,
  created_at TIMESTAMPTZ DEFAULT NOW(),
  updated_at TIMESTAMPTZ DEFAULT NOW()
```

);
```

## DynamoDB Schema for Real-Time Activity:

### 1. Activities Table:

- `activity_id`: Primary Key (UUID)

- `user_id`: Partition Key (String)

- `activity_type`: Activity Type (String)

- `timestamp`: Sort Key (Number)

- `details`: JSON String for Additional Information

```json
{
  "TableName": "Activities",
  "KeySchema": [
    { "AttributeName": "user_id", "KeyType": "HASH" },
    { "AttributeName": "timestamp", "KeyType": "RANGE" }
  ],
  "AttributeDefinitions": [

```
    { "AttributeName": "user_id", "AttributeType": "S"
},
    { "AttributeName": "timestamp", "AttributeType": "N" }
  ],
  "ProvisionedThroughput": {
    "ReadCapacityUnits": 5,
    "WriteCapacityUnits": 5
  }
```

Building RESTful API

We will use Python's Flask framework to build a RESTful API that will interact with both PostgreSQL and DynamoDB.

Setting Up the Environment

First, install the necessary packages:

```bash
pip install Flask psycopg2-binary boto3
```

Configuring the Flask Application

Create a file named `app.py`:

```python
from flask import Flask, request, jsonify
import psycopg2
import boto3
import uuid
from datetime import datetime

app = Flask(__name__)

# PostgreSQL connection setup
pg_conn = psycopg2.connect(
    dbname='your_db',
    user='your_user',
    password='your_password',
    host='your_host',
    port='your_port'
)
pg_conn.autocommit = True
pg_cursor = pg_conn.cursor()

# DynamoDB connection setup
dynamodb = boto3.resource('dynamodb', region_name='your_region')
activities_table = dynamodb.Table('Activities')
```

Creating API Endpoints

Endpoint to Create User:

```python
@app.route('/users', methods=['POST'])
def create_user():
    data = request.json
    user_id = str(uuid.uuid4())
    query = """
    INSERT INTO users (id, username, email)
    VALUES (%s, %s, %s)
    RETURNING id, username, email, created_at, updated_at;
    """
    pg_cursor.execute(query, (user_id, data['username'], data['email']))
    user = pg_cursor.fetchone()
    return jsonify({
        'id': user[0],
        'username': user[1],
        'email': user[2],
        'created_at': user[3],
        'updated_at': user[4]
    }), 201
```

Endpoint to Get User Profile:

```python
@app.route('/users/<user_id>', methods=['GET'])
def get_user_profile(user_id):
    query = """
    SELECT u.id, u.username, u.email, u.created_at, u.updated_at,
           p.first_name, p.last_name, p.date_of_birth, p.bio
    FROM users u
    LEFT JOIN profiles p ON u.id = p.user_id
    WHERE u.id = %s;
    """
    pg_cursor.execute(query, (user_id,))
    user_profile = pg_cursor.fetchone()
    if user_profile:
        return jsonify({
            'id': user_profile[0],
            'username': user_profile[1],
            'email': user_profile[2],
            'created_at': user_profile[3],
            'updated_at': user_profile[4],
            'first_name': user_profile[5],
            'last_name': user_profile[6],
            'date_of_birth': user_profile[7],
            'bio': user_profile[8]
        })
    return jsonify({'error': 'User not found'}), 404
```

Endpoint to Record Activity:

```python
@app.route('/activities', methods=['POST'])
def record_activity():
    data = request.json
    activity_id = str(uuid.uuid4())
    timestamp = int(datetime.now().timestamp())
    item = {
        'activity_id': activity_id,
        'user_id': data['user_id'],
        'activity_type': data['activity_type'],
        'timestamp': timestamp,
        'details': data.get('details', {})
    }
    activities_table.put_item(Item=item)
    return jsonify({'activity_id': activity_id}), 201
```

Endpoint to Get Activities for a User:

```python
@app.route('/activities/<user_id>', methods=['GET'])
def get_activities(user_id):
    response = activities_table.query(

KeyConditionExpression=boto3.dynamodb.conditions.Key('user_id').eq(user_id)
```

```
    )
    activities = response.get('Items', [])
    return jsonify(activities)
```

Testing the API

1. Create User:

```bash
curl -X POST -H "Content-Type: application/json" -d '{"username":"johndoe", "email":"johndoe@example.com"}' http://localhost:5000/users
```

2. Get User Profile:

```bash
curl -X GET http://localhost:5000/users/<user_id>
```

3. Record Activity:

```bash
curl -X POST -H "Content-Type: application/json" -d '{"user_id":"<user_id>", "activity_type":"login",
```

```
"details": {"ip": "192.168.1.1"}}'
http://localhost:5000/activities
```

4. Get Activities for a User:

```bash
curl -X GET http://localhost:5000/activities/<user_id>
```

By using PostgreSQL and DynamoDB together, we can optimize our application's data storage and retrieval processes. PostgreSQL handles structured, relational data efficiently, while DynamoDB excels in managing high-velocity, real-time activity data. The RESTful API built with Flask serves as an interface for interacting with these databases, providing a seamless experience for users and developers alike.

This approach ensures that user profiles are managed with strong consistency and transactional support, while real-time activities are handled with low latency and high scalability. This hybrid architecture leverages the strengths of both databases, ensuring optimal performance and reliability for your application.

Building Endpoints for User Management: User Registration, Login, and Profile Management (PostgreSQL)

User management is a critical component of many web applications, providing the foundational functionalities for user registration, login, and profile management. This article explores how to build these endpoints using PostgreSQL as the database and Flask for the RESTful API.

Setting Up the Environment

First, install the necessary packages:

```bash
pip install Flask psycopg2-binary bcrypt jwt
```

Configuring the Flask Application

Create a file named `app.py`:

```python
from flask import Flask, request, jsonify
import psycopg2
import bcrypt
import jwt
```

```python
import uuid
from datetime import datetime, timedelta

app = Flask(__name__)
app.config['SECRET_KEY'] = 'your_secret_key'

# PostgreSQL connection setup
pg_conn = psycopg2.connect(
    dbname='your_db',
    user='your_user',
    password='your_password',
    host='your_host',
    port='your_port'
)
pg_conn.autocommit = True
pg_cursor = pg_conn.cursor()

# Utility function to hash passwords
def hash_password(password):
    return bcrypt.hashpw(password.encode('utf-8'), bcrypt.gensalt())

# Utility function to check passwords
def check_password(hashed_password, password):
    return bcrypt.checkpw(password.encode('utf-8'), hashed_password)
```

User Registration

User registration involves creating a new user record in the database with a hashed password for security.

PostgreSQL Schema:

```sql
CREATE TABLE users (
  id UUID PRIMARY KEY DEFAULT gen_random_uuid(),
    username VARCHAR(50) UNIQUE NOT NULL,
    email VARCHAR(100) UNIQUE NOT NULL,
    password TEXT NOT NULL,
    created_at TIMESTAMPTZ DEFAULT NOW(),
    updated_at TIMESTAMPTZ DEFAULT NOW()
);

CREATE TABLE profiles (
  id UUID PRIMARY KEY DEFAULT gen_random_uuid(),
    user_id UUID REFERENCES users(id) ON DELETE CASCADE,
    first_name VARCHAR(50),
    last_name VARCHAR(50),
    date_of_birth DATE,
    bio TEXT,
    created_at TIMESTAMPTZ DEFAULT NOW(),
```

```
    updated_at TIMESTAMPTZ DEFAULT NOW()
);
```

API Endpoint:

```python
@app.route('/register', methods=['POST'])
def register_user():
    data = request.json
    user_id = str(uuid.uuid4())
    hashed_password = hash_password(data['password'])
    query = """
    INSERT INTO users (id, username, email, password)
    VALUES (%s, %s, %s, %s)
    RETURNING id, username, email, created_at, updated_at;
    """
    try:
        pg_cursor.execute(query, (user_id, data['username'], data['email'], hashed_password))
        user = pg_cursor.fetchone()
        return jsonify({
            'id': user[0],
            'username': user[1],
            'email': user[2],
            'created_at': user[3],
            'updated_at': user[4]
```

```
        }), 201
    except psycopg2.IntegrityError:
        return jsonify({'error': 'Username or email already exists'}), 409
```

User Login

User login involves verifying the username/email and password, and generating a JWT token upon successful authentication.

API Endpoint:

```python
@app.route('/login', methods=['POST'])
def login_user():
    data = request.json
    query = "SELECT id, username, email, password FROM users WHERE email = %s;"
    pg_cursor.execute(query, (data['email'],))
    user = pg_cursor.fetchone()
    if user and check_password(user[3], data['password']):
        token = jwt.encode({
            'user_id': user[0],
            'exp': datetime.utcnow() + timedelta(hours=1)
        }, app.config['SECRET_KEY'])
        return jsonify({'token': token})
```

```
        return jsonify({'error': 'Invalid credentials'}), 401
```

Profile Management

Profile management involves CRUD operations on the user's profile. For simplicity, we'll focus on creating and retrieving profiles.

API Endpoint to Create Profile:

```python
@app.route('/profile', methods=['POST'])
def create_profile():
    token = request.headers.get('Authorization').split()[1]
    try:
        decoded = jwt.decode(token, app.config['SECRET_KEY'], algorithms=["HS256"])
        user_id = decoded['user_id']
    except jwt.ExpiredSignatureError:
        return jsonify({'error': 'Token expired'}), 401
    except jwt.InvalidTokenError:
        return jsonify({'error': 'Invalid token'}), 401

    data = request.json
    profile_id = str(uuid.uuid4())
    query = """
```

```
    INSERT INTO profiles (id, user_id, first_name,
last_name, date_of_birth, bio)
    VALUES (%s, %s, %s, %s, %s, %s)
    RETURNING id, first_name, last_name,
date_of_birth, bio, created_at, updated_at;
    """
    pg_cursor.execute(query, (profile_id, user_id,
data['first_name'], data['last_name'],
data['date_of_birth'], data['bio']))
    profile = pg_cursor.fetchone()
    return jsonify({
       'id': profile[0],
       'first_name': profile[1],
       'last_name': profile[2],
       'date_of_birth': profile[3],
       'bio': profile[4],
       'created_at': profile[5],
       'updated_at': profile[6]
    }), 201
```

API Endpoint to Get Profile:

```python
@app.route('/profile', methods=['GET'])
def get_profile():
    token = request.headers.get('Authorization').split()[1]
    try:
```

```
        decoded = jwt.decode(token,
app.config['SECRET_KEY'], algorithms=["HS256"])
        user_id = decoded['user_id']
    except jwt.ExpiredSignatureError:
        return jsonify({'error': 'Token expired'}), 401
    except jwt.InvalidTokenError:
        return jsonify({'error': 'Invalid token'}), 401

    query = """
    SELECT p.id, p.first_name, p.last_name,
p.date_of_birth, p.bio, p.created_at, p.updated_at
    FROM profiles p
    WHERE p.user_id = %s;
    """
    pg_cursor.execute(query, (user_id,))
    profile = pg_cursor.fetchone()
    if profile:
        return jsonify({
            'id': profile[0],
            'first_name': profile[1],
            'last_name': profile[2],
            'date_of_birth': profile[3],
            'bio': profile[4],
            'created_at': profile[5],
            'updated_at': profile[6]
        })
    return jsonify({'error': 'Profile not found'}), 404
```

Updating and Deleting Profiles

API Endpoint to Update Profile:

```python
@app.route('/profile', methods=['PUT'])
def update_profile():
    token = request.headers.get('Authorization').split()[1]
    try:
        decoded = jwt.decode(token, app.config['SECRET_KEY'], algorithms=["HS256"])
        user_id = decoded['user_id']
    except jwt.ExpiredSignatureError:
        return jsonify({'error': 'Token expired'}), 401
    except jwt.InvalidTokenError:
        return jsonify({'error': 'Invalid token'}), 401

    data = request.json
    query = """
    UPDATE profiles SET first_name = %s, last_name = %s, date_of_birth = %s, bio = %s, updated_at = NOW()
    WHERE user_id = %s
    RETURNING id, first_name, last_name, date_of_birth, bio, created_at, updated_at;
    """
```

```
    pg_cursor.execute(query, (data['first_name'], data['last_name'], data['date_of_birth'], data['bio'], user_id))
    profile = pg_cursor.fetchone()
    if profile:
        return jsonify({
            'id': profile[0],
            'first_name': profile[1],
            'last_name': profile[2],
            'date_of_birth': profile[3],
            'bio': profile[4],
            'created_at': profile[5],
            'updated_at': profile[6]
        })
    return jsonify({'error': 'Profile not found'}), 404
```

API Endpoint to Delete Profile:

```python
@app.route('/profile', methods=['DELETE'])
def delete_profile():
    token = request.headers.get('Authorization').split()[1]
    try:
        decoded = jwt.decode(token, app.config['SECRET_KEY'], algorithms=["HS256"])
        user_id = decoded['user_id']
    except jwt.ExpiredSignatureError:
```

```
        return jsonify({'error': 'Token expired'}), 401
    except jwt.InvalidTokenError:
        return jsonify({'error': 'Invalid token'}), 401

    query = "DELETE FROM profiles WHERE user_id = %s RETURNING id;"
    pg_cursor.execute(query, (user_id,))
    profile = pg_cursor.fetchone()
    if profile:
        return jsonify({'message': 'Profile deleted successfully'})
    return jsonify({'error': 'Profile not found'}), 404
```

Full Application Code

For a complete view, here is the entire application code:

```python
from flask import Flask, request, jsonify
import psycopg2
import bcrypt
import jwt
import uuid
from datetime import datetime, timedelta

app = Flask(__name__)
app.config['SECRET_KEY'] = 'your_secret_key'
```

```python
# PostgreSQL connection setup
pg_conn = psycopg2.connect(
    dbname='your_db',
    user='your_user',
    password='your_password',
    host='your_host',
    port='your_port'
)
pg_conn.autocommit =```python
True
pg_cursor = pg_conn.cursor()

# Utility function to hash passwords
def hash_password(password):
    return bcrypt.hashpw(password.encode('utf-8'), bcrypt.gensalt())

# Utility function to check passwords
def check_password(hashed_password, password):
    return bcrypt.checkpw(password.encode('utf-8'), hashed_password)

@app.route('/register', methods=['POST'])
def register_user():
    data = request.json
    user_id = str(uuid.uuid4())
    hashed_password = hash_password(data['password'])
```

```python
    query = """
    INSERT INTO users (id, username, email, password)
    VALUES (%s, %s, %s, %s)
    RETURNING id, username, email, created_at, updated_at;
    """
    try:
        pg_cursor.execute(query, (user_id, data['username'], data['email'], hashed_password))
        user = pg_cursor.fetchone()
        return jsonify({
            'id': user[0],
            'username': user[1],
            'email': user[2],
            'created_at': user[3],
            'updated_at': user[4]
        }), 201
    except psycopg2.IntegrityError:
        return jsonify({'error': 'Username or email already exists'}), 409

@app.route('/login', methods=['POST'])
def login_user():
    data = request.json
    query = "SELECT id, username, email, password FROM users WHERE email = %s;"
    pg_cursor.execute(query, (data['email'],))
    user = pg_cursor.fetchone()
```

```
        if user and check_password(user[3], data['password']):
            token = jwt.encode({
                'user_id': user[0],
                'exp': datetime.utcnow() + timedelta(hours=1)
            }, app.config['SECRET_KEY'])
            return jsonify({'token': token})
        return jsonify({'error': 'Invalid credentials'}), 401


    @app.route('/profile', methods=['POST'])
    def create_profile():
        token = request.headers.get('Authorization').split()[1]
        try:
            decoded = jwt.decode(token, app.config['SECRET_KEY'], algorithms=["HS256"])
            user_id = decoded['user_id']
        except jwt.ExpiredSignatureError:
            return jsonify({'error': 'Token expired'}), 401
        except jwt.InvalidTokenError:
            return jsonify({'error': 'Invalid token'}), 401

        data = request.json
        profile_id = str(uuid.uuid4())
        query = """
        INSERT INTO profiles (id, user_id, first_name, last_name, date_of_birth, bio)
            VALUES (%s, %s, %s, %s, %s, %s)
            RETURNING id, first_name, last_name, date_of_birth, bio, created_at, updated_at;
```

```
    """

    pg_cursor.execute(query, (profile_id, user_id,
data['first_name'], data['last_name'],
data['date_of_birth'], data['bio']))
    profile = pg_cursor.fetchone()
    return jsonify({
        'id': profile[0],
        'first_name': profile[1],
        'last_name': profile[2],
        'date_of_birth': profile[3],
        'bio': profile[4],
        'created_at': profile[5],
        'updated_at': profile[6]
    }), 201

@app.route('/profile', methods=['GET'])
def get_profile():
    token = request.headers.get('Authorization').split()[1]
    try:
        decoded = jwt.decode(token, app.config['SECRET_KEY'], algorithms=["HS256"])
        user_id = decoded['user_id']
    except jwt.ExpiredSignatureError:
        return jsonify({'error': 'Token expired'}), 401
    except jwt.InvalidTokenError:
        return jsonify({'error': 'Invalid token'}), 401

    query = """
```

```
    SELECT p.id, p.first_name, p.last_name,
p.date_of_birth, p.bio, p.created_at, p.updated_at
    FROM profiles p
    WHERE p.user_id = %s;
    """
    pg_cursor.execute(query, (user_id,))
    profile = pg_cursor.fetchone()
    if profile:
        return jsonify({
            'id': profile[0],
            'first_name': profile[1],
            'last_name': profile[2],
            'date_of_birth': profile[3],
            'bio': profile[4],
            'created_at': profile[5],
            'updated_at': profile[6]
        })
    return jsonify({'error': 'Profile not found'}), 404

@app.route('/profile', methods=['PUT'])
def update_profile():
    token = request.headers.get('Authorization').split()[1]
    try:
        decoded = jwt.decode(token, app.config['SECRET_KEY'], algorithms=["HS256"])
        user_id = decoded['user_id']
    except jwt.ExpiredSignatureError:
        return jsonify({'error': 'Token expired'}), 401
```

```
    except jwt.InvalidTokenError:
        return jsonify({'error': 'Invalid token'}), 401

    data = request.json
    query = """
    UPDATE profiles SET first_name = %s, last_name = %s, date_of_birth = %s, bio = %s, updated_at = NOW()
    WHERE user_id = %s
    RETURNING id, first_name, last_name, date_of_birth, bio, created_at, updated_at;
    """
    pg_cursor.execute(query, (data['first_name'], data['last_name'], data['date_of_birth'], data['bio'], user_id))
    profile = pg_cursor.fetchone()
    if profile:
        return jsonify({
            'id': profile[0],
            'first_name': profile[1],
            'last_name': profile[2],
            'date_of_birth': profile[3],
            'bio': profile[4],
            'created_at': profile[5],
            'updated_at': profile[6]
        })
    return jsonify({'error': 'Profile not found'}), 404

@app.route('/profile', methods=['DELETE'])
```

```
def delete_profile():
    token = request.headers.get('Authorization').split()[1]
    try:
        decoded = jwt.decode(token, app.config['SECRET_KEY'], algorithms=["HS256"])
        user_id = decoded['user_id']
    except jwt.ExpiredSignatureError:
        return jsonify({'error': 'Token expired'}), 401
    except jwt.InvalidTokenError:
        return jsonify({'error': 'Invalid token'}), 401

    query = "DELETE FROM profiles WHERE user_id = %s RETURNING id;"
    pg_cursor.execute(query, (user_id,))
    profile = pg_cursor.fetchone()
    if profile:
        return jsonify({'message': 'Profile deleted successfully'})
    return jsonify({'error': 'Profile not found'}), 404

if __name__ == '__main__':
    app.run(debug=True)
```

In this article, we explored how to build endpoints for user registration, login, and profile management using PostgreSQL as the database and Flask for the RESTful API. These endpoints provide essential functionalities for user management, ensuring secure user authentication and enabling users to manage their profiles effectively. With these endpoints in place, you can create robust web applications with user management capabilities, laying the foundation for further feature development and user engagement.

Implementing Real-Time Features: Notifications and Updates powered by DynamoDB

Implementing real-time features like notifications and updates powered by DynamoDB requires a comprehensive understanding of both DynamoDB and the mechanisms for real-time data processing. In this guide, we'll walk through the steps to build a RESTful API using DynamoDB, and then integrate real-time features such as notifications and updates.

Setting up DynamoDB

First, let's set up DynamoDB. You can do this through the AWS Management Console or programmatically using AWS SDKs. Ensure you have the necessary permissions and access keys.

Building the RESTful API

We'll build a simple RESTful API using a serverless framework like AWS Lambda and API Gateway.

1. Define API Endpoints: Define the endpoints for CRUD operations on your DynamoDB tables. For example:

- `GET /items`: Retrieve all items

- `GET /items/{id}`: Retrieve a specific item

- `POST /items`: Create a new item

- `PUT /items/{id}`: Update an existing item

- `DELETE /items/{id}`: Delete an item

2. Implement Lambda Functions: Write Lambda functions to handle the business logic for each endpoint. These functions will interact with DynamoDB to perform CRUD operations.

3. Set up API Gateway: Create an API Gateway to route HTTP requests to the corresponding Lambda functions based on the endpoint.

4. Test the API: Test the API endpoints using tools like Postman to ensure they work as expected.

Adding Real-Time Features

Now, let's integrate real-time features such as notifications and updates into our API using DynamoDB Streams and AWS Lambda.

1. Enable DynamoDB Streams: Enable DynamoDB Streams on the tables you want to monitor for changes. This will capture insert, update, and delete events.

2. Write Lambda Function for Real-Time Processing: Create a Lambda function that listens to DynamoDB Streams. This function will be triggered whenever there's a change in the DynamoDB table.

3. Implement Notification Logic: Inside the Lambda function, implement logic to send notifications based on the changes. For example, if a new item is added to the table, send a notification to all subscribed users.

4. Update Logic: Similarly, implement logic to handle updates. For example, if an item is updated, broadcast the changes to relevant users in real-time.

Example Code:

Let's implement a simplified version of the above steps using Node.js and AWS SDK:

```javascript
// Lambda function to handle DynamoDB Streams
exports.handler = async (event) => {
    console.log('Received event:', JSON.stringify(event, null, 2));

    // Iterate through records
    for (const record of event.Records) {
        // Extract data from the record
        const { eventName, dynamodb } = record;
        const { NewImage, OldImage } = dynamodb;

        // Implement logic based on the eventName (INSERT, MODIFY, REMOVE)
        switch(eventName) {
            case 'INSERT':
                // Send notification for new item
                await sendNotification('New item added: ' + JSON.stringify(NewImage));
                break;
            case 'MODIFY':
                // Broadcast update to relevant users
                await broadcastUpdate('Item updated: ' + JSON.stringify(NewImage));
                break;
```

```
    case 'REMOVE':
      // Handle deletion
      break;
    default:
      break;
  };

// Function to send notification
async function sendNotification(message) {
  // Implement notification logic (e.g., send email, push notification)
}

// Function to broadcast update
async function broadcastUpdate(message) {
  // Implement broadcast logic (e.g., WebSocket, SSE)
}
```

Implementing real-time features like notifications and updates powered by DynamoDB adds a new dimension to your application, enhancing user experience and engagement. By leveraging DynamoDB Streams and AWS Lambda, you can build scalable and efficient real-time systems that react to changes in your data in milliseconds.

Securing Your Social Media Platform: Authentication and Authorization Strategies

Securing a social media platform is crucial to protect user data and ensure a safe and trusted environment for users. In this guide, we'll discuss authentication and authorization strategies for securing your social media platform's RESTful API, based on DynamoDB and PostgreSQL.

Authentication Strategies

Authentication verifies the identity of users accessing your platform. Here are some authentication strategies you can implement:

1. Token-Based Authentication (JWT): Use JSON Web Tokens (JWT) to authenticate users. When a user logs in, generate a JWT containing user information and send it to the client. The client includes the JWT in subsequent requests to access protected resources.

2. OAuth 2.0: Implement OAuth 2.0 for third-party authentication. Users can log in using their existing accounts from providers like Google, Facebook, or Twitter. OAuth 2.0 allows secure authorization without sharing credentials.

3. Session-Based Authentication: Use session-based authentication with cookies. When a user logs in, create a session identifier stored in a cookie on the client-side. Validate the session identifier on subsequent requests.

Authorization Strategies

Authorization controls what authenticated users can do within your platform. Here are some authorization strategies:

1. Role-Based Access Control (RBAC): Assign roles to users (e.g., admin, moderator, regular user) and define permissions associated with each role. Restrict access to certain endpoints or actions based on the user's role.

2. Attribute-Based Access Control (ABAC): Implement access control based on user attributes (e.g., age, location, subscription level). Define policies that evaluate user attributes to determine access rights.

3. Resource-Based Access Control: Control access to specific resources (e.g., posts, comments, user profiles) based on ownership or relationships. Users can only access resources they own or have permission to access.

Example Implementation

Let's implement token-based authentication and role-based authorization using Node.js, Express, and Passport.js with JWT strategy:

```javascript
const express = require('express');
const passport = require('passport');
const jwt = require('jsonwebtoken');
const bcrypt = require('bcrypt');
const { Strategy: JwtStrategy, ExtractJwt } = require('passport-jwt');

const app = express();

// Configure Passport
passport.use(new JwtStrategy({
   jwtFromRequest: ExtractJwt.fromAuthHeaderAsBearerToken(),
   secretOrKey: 'your_secret_key'
}, (payload, done) => {
   // Verify JWT payload and find user in database
   const user = getUserById(payload.sub);
   if (user) {
      return done(null, user);
   } else {
      return done(null, false);
   }
}));
```

```javascript
// Login Route
app.post('/login', async (req, res) => {
  const { email, password } = req.body;
  // Authenticate user
  const user = await authenticateUser(email, password);
  if (user) {
    // Generate JWT
    const token = jwt.sign({ sub: user.id }, 'your_secret_key', { expiresIn: '1h' });
    res.json({ token });
  } else {
    res.status(401).json({ message: 'Invalid credentials' });
  }
});

// Protected Route
app.get('/profile', passport.authenticate('jwt', { session: false }), (req, res) => {
  res.json(req.user);
});

// Role-based authorization middleware
function isAdmin(req, res, next) {
  if (req.user.role === 'admin') {
    return next();
  } else {
    return res.status(403).json({ message: 'Access forbidden' });
```

```
}

// Admin-only Route
app.get('/admin', passport.authenticate('jwt', { session:
false }), isAdmin, (req, res) => {
  res.json({ message: 'Admin dashboard' });
});

// Start server
app.listen(3000, () => {
  console.log('Server is running on port 3000');
});
```

Securing your social media platform is essential to protect user data and maintain user trust. Implementing robust authentication and authorization strategies like token-based authentication and role-based access control ensures that only authorized users can access your platform's resources. By combining these strategies with careful design and implementation, you can create a secure and trusted environment for your users.

Building a High-Traffic E-Commerce Platform: Balancing Product Catalog (PostgreSQL) with Shopping Cart and Order Processing (DynamoDB)

Building a high-traffic e-commerce platform involves meticulous planning, efficient architecture, and the right technology stack. Balancing the product catalog, shopping cart, and order processing is critical for ensuring seamless user experience and scalability. In this guide, we'll explore how to build such a platform using PostgreSQL for the product catalog and DynamoDB for shopping cart and order processing, with a focus on building RESTful APIs.

Introduction to the Technology Stack:

PostgreSQL:

PostgreSQL is a powerful, open-source relational database management system known for its reliability, robustness, and extensibility. It's well-suited for managing structured data such as product information, user data, and inventory.

DynamoDB:

DynamoDB is a fully managed NoSQL database service provided by Amazon Web Services (AWS). It offers seamless scalability, high performance, and low latency, making it an ideal choice for handling high-volume, unpredictable workloads like shopping carts and order processing.

RESTful API:

RESTful APIs provide a standardized way for different software applications to communicate over HTTP. They are stateless, scalable, and easy to integrate, making them the preferred choice for building modern web applications, including e-commerce platforms.

Architecture Overview:

Our e-commerce platform will consist of the following components:

1. Frontend Application: The user interface where customers can browse products, add items to their cart, and complete purchases.

2. RESTful API Layer: Serves as the intermediary between the frontend application and the databases, handling requests for product information, shopping cart operations, and order processing.

3. PostgreSQL Database: Stores the product catalog, user information, and inventory data.

4. DynamoDB: Manages shopping carts and order information.

Setting Up the Development Environment:

Let's start by setting up our development environment and installing the necessary dependencies:

```bash
# Install Node.js and npm
sudo apt install nodejs npm

# Install Express.js framework for building APIs
npm install express --save

# Install AWS SDK for interacting with DynamoDB
npm install aws-sdk --save

# Install pg-promise for PostgreSQL database connectivity
npm install pg-promise --save
```

Creating RESTful API Endpoints:

We'll create RESTful API endpoints to handle CRUD (Create, Read, Update, Delete) operations for products, shopping carts, and orders.

Product Endpoints:

```javascript
// productRoutes.js

const express = require('express');
const router = express.Router();

// Import PostgreSQL database connection
const db = require('../db');

// Get all products
router.get('/products', async (req, res) => {
  try {
    const products = await db.any('SELECT * FROM products');
    res.json(products);
  } catch (error) {
    console.error('Error fetching products:', error);
    res.status(500).json({ error: 'Internal server error' });
  }
});

// Add a new product
```

```javascript
router.post('/products', async (req, res) => {
  const { name, price, description } = req.body;
  try {
    await db.none('INSERT INTO products(name, price, description) VALUES($1, $2, $3)', [name, price, description]);
    res.json({ message: 'Product added successfully' });
  } catch (error) {
    console.error('Error adding product:', error);
    res.status(500).json({ error: 'Internal server error' });
  }
});

// Other CRUD endpoints for products (update and delete)
```

Shopping Cart Endpoints:

```javascript
// cartRoutes.js

const express = require('express');
const router = express.Router();

// Import AWS SDK for DynamoDB
const AWS = require('aws-sdk');
const dynamodb = new AWS.DynamoDB.DocumentClient();
```

```javascript
// Add item to shopping cart
router.post('/cart/add', async (req, res) => {
  const { userId, productId, quantity } = req.body;
  const params = {
    TableName: 'shopping_carts',
    Item: {
      userId,
      productId,
      quantity
    }
  };
  try {
    await dynamodb.put(params).promise();
    res.json({ message: 'Item added to cart successfully' });
  } catch (error) {
    console.error('Error adding item to cart:', error);
    res.status(500).json({ error: 'Internal server error' });
  }
});

// Other endpoints for updating and deleting items from the shopping cart
```

Order Processing Endpoints:

```javascript
// orderRoutes.js
```

```javascript
const express = require('express');
const router = express.Router();

// Import AWS SDK for DynamoDB
const AWS = require('aws-sdk');
const dynamodb = new AWS.DynamoDB.DocumentClient();

// Place order
router.post('/orders/place', async (req, res) => {
  const { userId, products } = req.body;
  const order = {
    userId,
    products,
    timestamp: Date.now()
  };
  const params = {
    TableName: 'orders',
    Item: order
  };
  try {
    await dynamodb.put(params).promise();
    res.json({ message: 'Order placed successfully' });
  } catch (error) {
    console.error('Error placing order:', error);
    res.status(500).json({ error: 'Internal server error' });
  }
});
```

// Other endpoints for retrieving order history, updating order status, etc.
```

By leveraging PostgreSQL for the product catalog and DynamoDB for shopping cart and order processing, we've created a scalable and efficient architecture for our high-traffic e-commerce platform. The RESTful APIs we've implemented facilitate seamless communication between the frontend application and the databases, enabling smooth user experience and efficient management of product catalog, shopping carts, and orders. This architecture can be further enhanced with features like caching, load balancing, and monitoring to ensure optimal performance and reliability.
```

Chapter 7

Building a Real-Time IoT Application: Collecting sensor data from devices (DynamoDB) and analyzing trends (PostgreSQL)

Building a real-time Internet of Things (IoT) application involves collecting sensor data from devices, storing it efficiently, and analyzing trends for insights. In this guide, we'll explore how to build such an application using DynamoDB for collecting sensor data and PostgreSQL for analyzing trends. We'll focus on building RESTful APIs to facilitate communication between the IoT devices and the databases.

Introduction to the Technology Stack:

DynamoDB:

DynamoDB is a fully managed NoSQL database service provided by Amazon Web Services (AWS). It offers seamless scalability, high performance, and low latency, making it an ideal choice for storing high-volume, time-series data generated by IoT devices.

PostgreSQL:

PostgreSQL is a powerful, open-source relational database management system known for its reliability, robustness, and extensibility. It's well-suited for performing complex analytical queries and generating insights from large datasets.

RESTful API:

RESTful APIs provide a standardized way for IoT devices to communicate with the databases over HTTP. They are stateless, scalable, and easy to integrate, making them the preferred choice for building modern IoT applications.

Architecture Overview:

Our real-time IoT application will consist of the following components:

1. IoT Devices: Sensors and devices that collect data and transmit it to the server.

2. RESTful API Layer: Serves as the intermediary between the IoT devices and the databases, handling requests for storing sensor data and analyzing trends.

3. DynamoDB: Stores raw sensor data collected from the devices.

4. PostgreSQL Database: Stores aggregated data and performs analytical queries to generate insights and trends.

Setting Up the Development Environment:

Let's start by setting up our development environment and installing the necessary dependencies:

```bash
# Install Node.js and npm
sudo apt install nodejs npm

# Install Express.js framework for building APIs
npm install express --save

# Install AWS SDK for interacting with DynamoDB
npm install aws-sdk --save

# Install pg-promise for PostgreSQL database connectivity
npm install pg-promise --save
```

Creating RESTful API Endpoints:

We'll create RESTful API endpoints to handle storing sensor data in DynamoDB and analyzing trends in PostgreSQL.

Sensor Data Endpoints:

```javascript
// sensorRoutes.js

const express = require('express');
const router = express.Router();

// Import AWS SDK for DynamoDB
const AWS = require('aws-sdk');
const dynamodb = new AWS.DynamoDB.DocumentClient();

// Add sensor data
router.post('/sensor/data', async (req, res) => {
  const { deviceId, timestamp, data } = req.body;
  const params = {
    TableName: 'sensor_data',
    Item: {
      deviceId,
      timestamp,
      data
    }
  };
  try {
```

```
    await dynamodb.put(params).promise();
    res.json({ message: 'Sensor data added successfully'
});
  } catch (error) {
    console.error('Error adding sensor data:', error);
    res.status(500).json({ error: 'Internal server error' });
});

// Other endpoints for retrieving sensor data, updating data, etc.
```

Trend Analysis Endpoints:

```javascript
// analysisRoutes.js

const express = require('express');
const router = express.Router();

// Import pg-promise for PostgreSQL database connectivity
const pgp = require('pg-promise')();
const db = pgp('postgres://username:password@localhost:5432/database');

// Analyze trends
```

```
router.get('/analysis/trends', async (req, res) => {
  try {
    // Perform analytical queries on PostgreSQL database
    const trends = await db.any('SELECT * FROM sensor_data WHERE ...');
    res.json(trends);
  } catch (error) {
    console.error('Error analyzing trends:', error);
    res.status(500).json({ error: 'Internal server error' });
  }
});

// Other endpoints for generating reports, forecasting, etc.
```

By leveraging DynamoDB for storing sensor data and PostgreSQL for analyzing trends, we've created a real-time IoT application capable of collecting, storing, and analyzing data from IoT devices. The RESTful APIs we've implemented facilitate seamless communication between the IoT devices and the databases, enabling efficient data collection and analysis. This architecture can be further enhanced with features like data preprocessing, anomaly detection, and real-time visualization to provide valuable insights and improve decision-making in various industries such as manufacturing, healthcare, agriculture, and smart cities.

Building a Scalable Content Management System: User-Generated Content and Media Files (DynamoDB) with Post Metadata (PostgreSQL)

Building a scalable Content Management System (CMS) involves managing user-generated content, media files, and post metadata efficiently. This guide explores how to build such a CMS using DynamoDB for user-generated content and media files and PostgreSQL for post metadata. We'll focus on building RESTful APIs to facilitate seamless communication between the front-end application and the databases.

Introduction to the Technology Stack:

DynamoDB:

DynamoDB is a fully managed NoSQL database service provided by Amazon Web Services (AWS). It offers seamless scalability, high performance, and low latency, making it an ideal choice for managing large volumes of user-generated content and media files.

PostgreSQL:

PostgreSQL is a powerful, open-source relational database management system known for its reliability, robustness, and extensibility. It's well-suited for managing structured data such as post metadata, user information, and relations between different entities.

RESTful API:

RESTful APIs provide a standardized way for different software applications to communicate over HTTP. They are stateless, scalable, and easy to integrate, making them the preferred choice for building modern web applications, including content management systems.

Architecture Overview:

Our scalable CMS will consist of the following components:

1. Frontend Application: The user interface where users can create, edit, and view content and media files.

2. RESTful API Layer: Serves as the intermediary between the frontend application and the databases, handling requests for managing content, media files, and post metadata.

3. DynamoDB: Stores user-generated content and media files.

4. PostgreSQL Database: Stores post metadata, user information, and relationships between different entities.

Setting Up the Development Environment:

Let's start by setting up our development environment and installing the necessary dependencies:

```bash
# Install Node.js and npm
sudo apt install nodejs npm

# Install Express.js framework for building APIs
npm install express --save

# Install AWS SDK for interacting with DynamoDB
npm install aws-sdk --save

# Install pg-promise for PostgreSQL database connectivity
npm install pg-promise --save
```

Creating RESTful API Endpoints:

We'll create RESTful API endpoints to handle CRUD (Create, Read, Update, Delete) operations for user-generated content, media files, and post metadata.

User-Generated Content and Media Files Endpoints:

```javascript
// contentRoutes.js

const express = require('express');
const router = express.Router();

// Import AWS SDK for DynamoDB
const AWS = require('aws-sdk');
const dynamodb = new AWS.DynamoDB.DocumentClient();

// Add user-generated content
router.post('/content', async (req, res) => {
  const { userId, contentId, content, mediaUrl, timestamp
} = req.body;
  const params = {
    TableName: 'user_content',
    Item: {
      userId,
      contentId,
      content,
      mediaUrl,
      timestamp
    }
  };
  try {
```

```
    await dynamodb.put(params).promise();
    res.json({ message: 'Content added successfully' });
  } catch (error) {
    console.error('Error adding content:', error);
    res.status(500).json({ error: 'Internal server error' });
  }
});

// Get user-generated content
router.get('/content/:contentId', async (req, res) => {
  const { contentId } = req.params;
  const params = {
    TableName: 'user_content',
    Key: { contentId }
  };
  try {
    const result = await dynamodb.get(params).promise();
    res.json(result.Item);
  } catch (error) {
    console.error('Error fetching content:', error);
    res.status(500).json({ error: 'Internal server error' });
  }
});

// Other CRUD endpoints for user-generated content and media files (update and delete)
```

Post Metadata Endpoints:

```javascript
// metadataRoutes.js

const express = require('express');
const router = express.Router();

// Import pg-promise for PostgreSQL database connectivity
const pgp = require('pg-promise')();
const db = pgp('postgres://username:password@localhost:5432/cms');

// Add post metadata
router.post('/metadata', async (req, res) => {
  const { postId, title, description, tags, userId } = req.body;
  try {
    await db.none('INSERT INTO post_metadata(post_id, title, description, tags, user_id) VALUES($1, $2, $3, $4, $5)', [postId, title, description, tags, userId]);
    res.json({ message: 'Metadata added successfully' });
  } catch (error) {
    console.error('Error adding metadata:', error);
    res.status(500).json({ error: 'Internal server error' });
  }
});

// Get post metadata
```

```
router.get('/metadata/:postId', async (req, res) => {
  const { postId } = req.params;
  try {
    const metadata = await db.one('SELECT * FROM post_metadata WHERE post_id = $1', [postId]);
    res.json(metadata);
  } catch (error) {
    console.error('Error fetching metadata:', error);
    res.status(500).json({ error: 'Internal server error' });
  }
});

// Other CRUD endpoints for post metadata (update and delete)
```

By leveraging DynamoDB for user-generated content and media files and PostgreSQL for post metadata, we've created a scalable and efficient architecture for our content management system. The RESTful APIs we've implemented facilitate seamless communication between the frontend application and the databases, enabling smooth user experience and efficient management of content and metadata.

Detailed Implementation:

Setting Up DynamoDB:

To set up DynamoDB, create a new table named `user_content` with the following attributes:

- **`userId` (Partition Key):** The unique identifier for the user.

- **`contentId` (Sort Key):** The unique identifier for the content.

```json
{
  "TableName": "user_content",
  "KeySchema": [
    { "AttributeName": "userId", "KeyType": "HASH" },
    { "AttributeName": "contentId", "KeyType": "RANGE" }
  ],
  "AttributeDefinitions": [
    { "AttributeName": "userId", "AttributeType": "S" },
    { "AttributeName": "contentId", "AttributeType": "S" }
  ],
  "ProvisionedThroughput": {
    "ReadCapacityUnits": 5,
    "WriteCapacityUnits": 5
  }
}
```

Setting Up PostgreSQL:

To set up PostgreSQL, create a new table named `post_metadata` with the following schema:

```sql
CREATE TABLE post_metadata (
  post_id SERIAL PRIMARY KEY,
  title VARCHAR(255) NOT NULL,
  description TEXT,
  tags TEXT[],
  user_id INT REFERENCES users(user_id)
);
```

Implementing the RESTful API:

1. Content Management Endpoints:

- `POST /content`: Adds new content to DynamoDB.

- `GET /content/:contentId`: Retrieves content from DynamoDB based on `contentId`.

- `PUT /content/:contentId`: Updates existing content in DynamoDB.

- `DELETE /content/:contentId`: Deletes content from DynamoDB.

2. **Metadata Management Endpoints:**

    - `POST /metadata`: Adds new metadata to PostgreSQL.

    - `GET /metadata/:postId`: Retrieves metadata from PostgreSQL based on `postId`.

    - `PUT /metadata/:postId`: Updates existing metadata in PostgreSQL.

    - `DELETE /metadata/:postId`: Deletes metadata from PostgreSQL.

Content Management Code:

```javascript
// contentRoutes.js

const express = require('express');
const router = express.Router();
const AWS = require('aws-sdk');
const dynamodb = new AWS.DynamoDB.DocumentClient();
```

```
// Add user-generated content
router.post('/content', async (req, res) => {
  const { userId, contentId, content, mediaUrl, timestamp
  } = req.body;
  const params = {
    TableName: 'user_content',
    Item: {
      userId,
      contentId,
      content,
      mediaUrl,
      timestamp
    }
  };
  try {
    await dynamodb.put(params).promise();
    res.json({ message: 'Content added successfully' });
  } catch (error) {
    console.error('Error adding content:', error);
    res.status(500).json({ error: 'Internal server error' });
  }
});

// Get user-generated content
router.get('/content/:contentId', async (req, res) => {
  const { contentId } = req.params;
  const params = {
    TableName: 'user_content',
    Key: { contentId }
  };
```

```javascript
  try {
    const result = await dynamodb.get(params).promise();
    res.json(result.Item);
  } catch (error) {
    console.error('Error fetching content:', error);
    res.status(500).json({ error: 'Internal server error' });
  }
});

// Update user-generated content
router.put('/content/:contentId', async (req, res) => {
  const { contentId } = req.params;
  const { content, mediaUrl } = req.body;
  const params = {
    TableName: 'user_content',
    Key: { contentId },
    UpdateExpression: 'set content = :content, mediaUrl = :mediaUrl',
    ExpressionAttributeValues: {
      ':content': content,
      ':mediaUrl': mediaUrl
    }
  };
  try {
    await dynamodb.update(params).promise();
    res.json({ message: 'Content updated successfully' });
  } catch (error) {
    console.error('Error updating content:', error);
    res.status(500).json({ error: 'Internal
```

```javascript
// Update user-generated content
router.put('/content/:contentId', async (req, res) => {
  const { contentId } = req.params;
  const { content, mediaUrl } = req.body;
  const params = {
    TableName: 'user_content',
    Key: { contentId },
    UpdateExpression: 'set content = :content, mediaUrl = :mediaUrl',
    ExpressionAttributeValues: {
      ':content': content,
      ':mediaUrl': mediaUrl
    }
  };
  try {
    await dynamodb.update(params).promise();
    res.json({ message: 'Content updated successfully' });
  } catch (error) {
    console.error('Error updating content:', error);
    res.status(500).json({ error: 'Internal server error' });
  }
});

// Delete user-generated content
router.delete('/content/:contentId', async (req, res) => {
  const { contentId } = req.params;
  const params = {
    TableName: 'user_content',
    Key: { contentId }
  };
```

```javascript
  try {
    await dynamodb.delete(params).promise();
    res.json({ message: 'Content deleted successfully' });
  } catch (error) {
    console.error('Error deleting content:', error);
    res.status(500).json({ error: 'Internal server error' });
  }
});

module.exports = router;
```

Metadata Management Code:

```javascript
// metadataRoutes.js

const express = require('express');
const router = express.Router();
const pgp = require('pg-promise')();
const db = pgp('postgres://username:password@localhost:5432/cms');

// Add post metadata
router.post('/metadata', async (req, res) => {
  const { postId, title, description, tags, userId } = req.body;
  try {
```

```javascript
    await db.none('INSERT INTO post_metadata(post_id, title, description, tags, user_id) VALUES($1, $2, $3, $4, $5)', [postId, title, description, tags, userId]);
    res.json({ message: 'Metadata added successfully' });
  } catch (error) {
    console.error('Error adding metadata:', error);
    res.status(500).json({ error: 'Internal server error' });
  }
});

// Get post metadata
router.get('/metadata/:postId', async (req, res) => {
  const { postId } = req.params;
  try {
    const metadata = await db.one('SELECT * FROM post_metadata WHERE post_id = $1', [postId]);
    res.json(metadata);
  } catch (error) {
    console.error('Error fetching metadata:', error);
    res.status(500).json({ error: 'Internal server error' });
  }
});

// Update post metadata
router.put('/metadata/:postId', async (req, res) => {
  const { postId } = req.params;
  const { title, description, tags } = req.body;
  try {
```

```
    await db.none('UPDATE post_metadata SET title = 
$1, description = $2, tags = $3 WHERE post_id = $4',
[title, description, tags, postId]);
    res.json({ message: 'Metadata updated successfully'
});
  } catch (error) {
    console.error('Error updating metadata:', error);
    res.status(500).json({ error: 'Internal server error' });
});

// Delete post metadata
router.delete('/metadata/:postId', async (req, res) => {
  const { postId } = req.params;
  try {
    await db.none('DELETE FROM post_metadata
WHERE post_id = $1', [postId]);
    res.json({ message: 'Metadata deleted successfully' });
  } catch (error) {
    console.error('Error deleting metadata:', error);
    res.status(500).json({ error: 'Internal server error' });
});

module.exports = router;
```

Putting It All Together

We now have two sets of routes: one for handling user-generated content and media files using DynamoDB, and another for managing post metadata using PostgreSQL. Next, we'll set up the main server file to combine these routes.

```javascript
// server.js

const express = require('express');
const bodyParser = require('body-parser');
const app = express();
const port = 3000;

// Middleware
app.use(bodyParser.json());

// Import routes
const contentRoutes = require('./contentRoutes');
const metadataRoutes = require('./metadataRoutes');

// Use routes
app.use('/api', contentRoutes);
app.use('/api', metadataRoutes);

// Start server
app.listen(port, () => {
  console.log(`Server running on port ${port}`);
```

});
```

## Summary and Benefits

By leveraging DynamoDB and PostgreSQL, we've created a scalable and efficient architecture for our content management system. This system handles large volumes of user-generated content and media files using DynamoDB, which is optimized for high throughput and low latency. Meanwhile, PostgreSQL is used to manage post metadata, providing robust querying capabilities and relational data management.

**Benefits**:

**1. Scalability:** DynamoDB automatically scales to handle large amounts of data and high request rates, making it ideal for managing user-generated content and media files.

**2. Performance:** PostgreSQL offers powerful indexing and querying capabilities, making it suitable for handling complex queries related to post metadata.

**3. Flexibility:** The RESTful API design allows for easy integration with various frontend frameworks and other services.
```

4. Separation of Concerns: By using different databases for content and metadata, we ensure that each database is optimized for its specific workload.

Future Enhancements:

1. Caching: Implement caching mechanisms using services like Redis to improve performance for frequently accessed data.

2. Search Functionality: Integrate a search engine like Elasticsearch to enable advanced search features across user-generated content and metadata.

3. Authentication and Authorization: Implement robust user authentication and authorization using OAuth or JWT to secure the API endpoints.

4. Monitoring and Logging: Use monitoring tools like AWS CloudWatch for DynamoDB and pgAdmin for PostgreSQL to monitor database performance and troubleshoot issues.

5. Data Preprocessing: Implement data preprocessing steps to clean and validate user-generated content before storing it in DynamoDB.

By following this guide, you can build a scalable, efficient, and flexible content management system that can handle large volumes of user-generated content and media files, while providing robust metadata management capabilities. This architecture is well-suited for modern web applications that require high performance and scalability.

Chapter 8

Authentication and Authorization: Implementing User Access Control Mechanisms in a RESTful API with DynamoDB and PostgreSQL

In the world of web development, securing your application is of paramount importance. Two key components in securing any application are authentication and authorization. These mechanisms ensure that users are who they claim to be and have permissions to access specific resources. This article will explore how to implement user access control mechanisms in a RESTful API using DynamoDB and PostgreSQL.

Authentication vs. Authorization

Before diving into the implementation, it's important to distinguish between authentication and authorization:

- **Authentication**: This is the process of verifying the identity of a user. It answers the question, "Who are you?"

- **Authorization**: This is the process of verifying what specific applications, files, and data a user has access to. It answers the question, "What can you do?"

Setting Up the Environment

To build our RESTful API with user access control mechanisms, we will use the following technologies:

- **Nodes.js:** A JavaScript runtime built on Chrome's V8 JavaScript engine.

- **Express.js:** A web application framework for Node.js.

- **DynamoDB**: A NoSQL database service provided by AWS.

- **PostgreSQL**: A powerful, open-source object-relational database system.

- **JSON Web Tokens (JWT)**: A compact, URL-safe means of representing claims to be transferred between two parties.

Step 1: Setting Up the Project

First, let's set up a new Node.js project:

```sh
mkdir user-access-control
cd user-access-control
npm init -y
npm install express body-parser jsonwebtoken bcryptjs pg aws-sdk
```

Step 2: Configuring DynamoDB and PostgreSQL

DynamoDB Configuration

Create a new file `dynamodb.js` to configure DynamoDB:

```js
const AWS = require('aws-sdk');

AWS.config.update({
  region: 'us-west-2',
  accessKeyId: 'YOUR_ACCESS_KEY_ID',
  secretAccessKey: 'YOUR_SECRET_ACCESS_KEY'
});

const dynamodb = new AWS.DynamoDB.DocumentClient();
```

```
module.exports = dynamodb;
```

PostgreSQL Configuration

Create a new file `database.js` to configure PostgreSQL:

```js
const { Pool } = require('pg');

const pool = new Pool({
  user: 'youruser',
  host: 'localhost',
  database: 'yourdb',
  password: 'yourpassword',
  port: 5432,
});

module.exports = pool;
```

Step 3: Implementing User Authentication

User Model

For user authentication, we need to create a user model. In our example, we'll use DynamoDB for storing user information.

Create a new file `models/User.js`:

```js
const dynamodb = require('../dynamodb');
const bcrypt = require('bcryptjs');
const jwt = require('jsonwebtoken');

const USERS_TABLE = 'Users';

class User {
  static async create({ username, password }) {
    const hashedPassword = await bcrypt.hash(password, 10);

    const params = {
      TableName: USERS_TABLE,
      Item: {
        username,
        password: hashedPassword,
      },
    };

    await dynamodb.put(params).promise();
  }
```

```javascript
  static async authenticate({ username, password }) {
    const params = {
      TableName: USERS_TABLE,
      Key: { username },
    };

    const result = await dynamodb.get(params).promise();

    if (!result.Item) {
      throw new Error('User not found');
    }

    const user = result.Item;

    const isPasswordValid = await bcrypt.compare(password, user.password);
    if (!isPasswordValid) {
      throw new Error('Invalid password');
    }

    const token = jwt.sign({ username }, 'secretkey', { expiresIn: '1h' });

    return { token };
  }

module.exports = User;
```

Authentication Routes

Create a new file `routes/auth.js` to handle authentication routes:

```js
const express = require('express');
const User = require('../models/User');

const router = express.Router();

router.post('/register', async (req, res) => {
  try {
    const { username, password } = req.body;
    await User.create({ username, password });
    res.status(201).send('User registered successfully');
  } catch (error) {
    res.status(400).send(error.message);
  }
});

router.post('/login', async (req, res) => {
  try {
    const { username, password } = req.body;
    const { token } = await User.authenticate({ username, password });
    res.status(200).json({ token });
  } catch (error) {
```

```
        res.status(400).send(error.message);
});

module.exports = router;
```

Step 4: Implementing User Authorization

Middleware for Authorization

To protect routes, we need to create a middleware that checks for a valid JWT token. Create a new file `middleware/auth.js`:

```js
const jwt = require('jsonwebtoken');

const auth = (req, res, next) => {
  const token = req.header('Authorization').replace('Bearer ', '');

  if (!token) {
    return res.status(401).send('Access denied. No token provided.');
  }

  try {
    const decoded = jwt.verify(token, 'secretkey');
```

```
    req.user = decoded;
    next();
  } catch (error) {
    res.status(400).send('Invalid token.');
};

module.exports = auth;
```

Protected Routes

Now, let's create some protected routes that only authenticated users can access. Create a new file `routes/protected.js`:

```js
const express = require('express');
const auth = require('../middleware/auth');

const router = express.Router();

router.get('/profile', auth, (req, res) => {
  res.send(`Welcome ${req.user.username}`);
});

module.exports = router;
```

Step 5: Integrating PostgreSQL for Additional Data Handling

In many applications, you might use DynamoDB for user data but PostgreSQL for relational data that needs complex queries. Let's integrate PostgreSQL for handling roles.

Roles Model

Create a new file `models/Role.js`:

```js
const pool = require('../database');

class Role {
  static async getUserRole(username) {
    const result = await pool.query('SELECT role FROM user_roles WHERE username = $1', [username]);
    return result.rows[0]?.role || null;
  }
}

module.exports = Role;
```

Authorization Middleware with Roles

Update the authorization middleware to include role checking. Modify `middleware/auth.js`:

```js
const jwt = require('jsonwebtoken');
const Role = require('../models/Role');

const auth = async (req, res, next) => {
  const token = req.header('Authorization').replace('Bearer ', '');

  if (!token) {
    return res.status(401).send('Access denied. No token provided.');
  }

  try {
    const decoded = jwt.verify(token, 'secretkey');
    req.user = decoded;

    const role = await Role.getUserRole(decoded.username);
    req.user.role = role;

    next();
  } catch (error) {
    res.status(400).send('Invalid token.');
  }
};
```

```
module.exports = auth;
```

Role-based Authorization

Create a middleware to check for specific roles:

```js
const roleAuthorization = (requiredRole) => {
  return (req, res, next) => {
    if (req.user.role !== requiredRole) {
      return res.status(403).send('Access denied. Insufficient permissions.');
    }
    next();
  };
};

module.exports = roleAuthorization;
```

Protected Routes with Role Authorization

Update `routes/protected.js` to include role-based authorization:

```js
const express = require('express');
```

```
const auth = require('../middleware/auth');
const roleAuthorization =
require('../middleware/roleAuthorization');

const router = express.Router();

router.get('/profile', auth, (req, res) => {
  res.send(`Welcome ${req.user.username}`);
});

router.get('/admin', auth, roleAuthorization('admin'),
(req, res) => {
  res.send('Welcome Admin');
});

module.exports = router;
```

Step 6: Setting Up the Server

Finally, set up the server in `index.js`:

```js
const express = require('express');
const bodyParser = require('body-parser');

const authRoutes = require('./routes/auth');
const protectedRoutes = require('./routes/protected');
```

```
const app = express();

app.use(bodyParser.json());

app.use('/auth', authRoutes);
app.use('/protected', protectedRoutes);

const port = process.env.PORT || 3000;
app.listen(port, () => {
  console.log(`Server running on port ${port}`);
});
```

In this article, we have covered the implementation of authentication and authorization mechanisms in a RESTful API using DynamoDB and PostgreSQL. By combining the strengths of both databases, we can build a robust and scalable user access control system. Authentication ensures that users are who they claim to be, while authorization determines what resources they can access. Using JWTs, we can securely transmit user credentials, and by leveraging middleware, we can protect routes and enforce role-based access control.

This setup provides a solid foundation for securing your application. Depending on your specific requirements, you might want to extend this system with more granular permissions, integrate additional security measures, or implement different authentication strategies.

Data Validation and Sanitization: Preventing Malicious Data Injection Attacks in a RESTful API with DynamoDB and PostgreSQL

In the realm of web development, safeguarding applications against malicious data injection attacks is crucial. Data validation and sanitization are fundamental techniques used to protect applications from these threats. This article explores the implementation of data validation and sanitization in a RESTful API using DynamoDB and PostgreSQL.

Understanding Data Injection Attacks

Data injection attacks, such as SQL injection and NoSQL injection, occur when an attacker manipulates input data to alter the execution of database queries. These attacks can lead to unauthorized data access, data corruption, and application compromise. Preventing these attacks involves validating and sanitizing all user inputs.

Setting Up the Environment

To build our RESTful API with data validation and sanitization, we will use the following technologies:

- **Node.js:** A JavaScript runtime built on Chrome's V8 JavaScript engine.

- **Express.js:** A web application framework for Node.js.

- **DynamoDB**: A NoSQL database service provided by AWS.

- **PostgreSQL**: A powerful, open-source object-relational database system.

- **Joi**: A powerful schema description language and data validator for JavaScript.

- **Express-validator:** A set of express.js middlewares that wraps validator.js.

- **pg**: PostgreSQL client for Node.js.

- **aws-sdk:** AWS SDK for JavaScript.

Step 1: Setting Up the Project

First, let's set up a new Node.js project:

```sh
mkdir data-validation-sanitization
cd data-validation-sanitization
npm init -y
npm install express body-parser joi express-validator pg aws-sdk
```

Step 2: Configuring DynamoDB and PostgreSQL

DynamoDB Configuration

Create a new file `dynamodb.js` to configure DynamoDB:

```js
const AWS = require('aws-sdk');

AWS.config.update({
  region: 'us-west-2',
  accessKeyId: 'YOUR_ACCESS_KEY_ID',
  secretAccessKey: 'YOUR_SECRET_ACCESS_KEY'
});

const dynamodb = new AWS.DynamoDB.DocumentClient();
```

```
module.exports = dynamodb;
```

PostgreSQL Configuration

Create a new file `database.js` to configure PostgreSQL:

```js
const { Pool } = require('pg');

const pool = new Pool({
  user: 'youruser',
  host: 'localhost',
  database: 'yourdb',
  password: 'yourpassword',
  port: 5432,
});

module.exports = pool;
```

Step 3: Implementing Data Validation and Sanitization

User Model

For our example, we'll use DynamoDB for user information and PostgreSQL for storing roles and other relational data.

Create a new file `models/User.js` for DynamoDB user model:

```js
const dynamodb = require('../dynamodb');
const bcrypt = require('bcryptjs');
const { v4: uuidv4 } = require('uuid');

const USERS_TABLE = 'Users';

class User {
  static async create({ username, password }) {
    const hashedPassword = await bcrypt.hash(password, 10);

    const params = {
      TableName: USERS_TABLE,
      Item: {
        userId: uuidv4(),
        username,
        password: hashedPassword,
      },
    };

    await dynamodb.put(params).promise();
```

```js
  }

  static async findByUsername(username) {
    const params = {
      TableName: USERS_TABLE,
      Key: { username },
    };

    const result = await dynamodb.get(params).promise();
    return result.Item;
  }
}

module.exports = User;
```

Role Model

Create a new file `models/Role.js` for PostgreSQL role model:

```js
const pool = require('../database');

class Role {
  static async getUserRole(username) {
    const result = await pool.query('SELECT role FROM user_roles WHERE username = $1', [username]);
    return result.rows[0]?.role || null;
```

}

```
module.exports = Role;
```

Step 4: Implementing Validation Middleware

Joi Validation

Create a new file `validators/user.js` to define validation schemas using Joi:

```js
const Joi = require('joi');

const registerSchema = Joi.object({
  username: Joi.string().alphanum().min(3).max(30).required(),
  password: Joi.string().min(8).required(),
});

const loginSchema = Joi.object({
  username: Joi.string().alphanum().min(3).max(30).required(),
  password: Joi.string().required(),
});

module.exports = { registerSchema, loginSchema };
```

```

Create a middleware to use these schemas in `middleware/validate.js`:

```js
const validate = (schema) => (req, res, next) => {
  const { error } = schema.validate(req.body);
  if (error) {
    return res.status(400).send(error.details[0].message);
  }
  next();
};

module.exports = validate;
```

Step 5: Implementing Authentication and Routes

Authentication Logic

Create a new file `controllers/auth.js`:

```js
const User = require('../models/User');
const bcrypt = require('bcryptjs');
const jwt = require('jsonwebtoken');
```
```

```javascript
const register = async (req, res) => {
  try {
    const { username, password } = req.body;
    const existingUser = await User.findByUsername(username);
    if (existingUser) {
      return res.status(400).send('User already exists');
    }

    await User.create({ username, password });
    res.status(201).send('User registered successfully');
  } catch (error) {
    res.status(500).send(error.message);
  }
};

const login = async (req, res) => {
  try {
    const { username, password } = req.body;
    const user = await User.findByUsername(username);
    if (!user) {
      return res.status(400).send('Invalid username or password');
    }

    const isPasswordValid = await bcrypt.compare(password, user.password);
    if (!isPasswordValid) {
```

```
    return res.status(400).send('Invalid username or password');
  }

  const token = jwt.sign({ username: user.username }, 'secretkey', { expiresIn: '1h' });
  res.status(200).json({ token });
  } catch (error) {
    res.status(500).send(error.message);
  }
};

module.exports = { register, login };
```

Authentication Routes

Create a new file `routes/auth.js` to handle authentication routes:

```js
const express = require('express');
const { register, login } = require('../controllers/auth');
const validate = require('../middleware/validate');
const { registerSchema, loginSchema } = require('../validators/user');

const router = express.Router();
```

```js
router.post('/register', validate(registerSchema), register);
router.post('/login', validate(loginSchema), login);

module.exports = router;
```

Step 6: Implementing Role-Based Authorization

Middleware for Role Authorization

Create a middleware to check for specific roles in `middleware/roleAuthorization.js`:

```js
const Role = require('../models/Role');

const roleAuthorization = (requiredRole) => {
  return async (req, res, next) => {
    const { username } = req.user;
    const userRole = await Role.getUserRole(username);

    if (userRole !== requiredRole) {
      return res.status(403).send('Access denied. Insufficient permissions.');
    }
    next();
  };
};
```

```
module.exports = roleAuthorization;
```

Middleware for JWT Authentication

Create a middleware to authenticate JWT tokens in `middleware/auth.js`:

```js
const jwt = require('jsonwebtoken');

const auth = (req, res, next) => {
  const token = req.header('Authorization').replace('Bearer ', '');
  if (!token) {
    return res.status(401).send('Access denied. No token provided.');
  }

  try {
    const decoded = jwt.verify(token, 'secretkey');
    req.user = decoded;
    next();
  } catch (error) {
    res.status(400).send('Invalid token.');
  }
};

module.exports = auth;
```

```

## Step 7: Creating Protected Routes

Create a new file `routes/protected.js` to handle protected routes:

```js
const express = require('express');
const auth = require('../middleware/auth');
const roleAuthorization =
require('../middleware/roleAuthorization');

const router = express.Router();

router.get('/profile', auth, (req, res) => {
  res.send(`Welcome ${req.user.username}`);
});

router.get('/admin', auth, roleAuthorization('admin'),
(req, res) => {
  res.send('Welcome Admin');
});

module.exports = router;
```

Step 8: Setting Up the Server
```

Finally, set up the server in `index.js`:

```js
const express = require('express');
const bodyParser = require('body-parser');

const authRoutes = require('./routes/auth');
const protectedRoutes = require('./routes/protected');

const app = express();

app.use(bodyParser.json());

app.use('/auth', authRoutes);
app.use('/protected', protectedRoutes);

const port = process.env.PORT || 3000;
app.listen(port, () => {
  console.log(`Server running on port ${port}`);
});
```

In this article, we have covered the implementation of data validation and sanitization in a RESTful API using DynamoDB and PostgreSQL. By integrating data validation and sanitization into our API, we can prevent malicious data injection attacks, ensuring the security and integrity of our application.

Data validation ensures that the data provided by users meets certain criteria before processing, while data sanitization ensures that the data is cleaned and formatted to prevent harmful content from causing security issues. By leveraging tools like Joi and express-validator, we can establish robust validation and sanitization mechanisms that help in safeguarding our application.

Detailed Implementation and Explanation

Let's go through the key components in more detail, highlighting how each part contributes to preventing data injection attacks.

1. Data Validation with Joi

Joi is a powerful library for validating data structures. Here's a more detailed explanation of our validation schemas:

`validators/user.js`:

```js
const Joi = require('joi');
```

```js
const registerSchema = Joi.object({
  username: Joi.string().alphanum().min(3).max(30).required(),
  password: Joi.string().min(8).required(),
});

const loginSchema = Joi.object({
  username: Joi.string().alphanum().min(3).max(30).required(),
  password: Joi.string().required(),
});

module.exports = { registerSchema, loginSchema };
```

- **username**: Ensures that the username is alphanumeric and between 3 to 30 characters.
- **password**: Ensures that the password is at least 8 characters long.

Middleware for Validation:

```js
const validate = (schema) => (req, res, next) => {
  const { error } = schema.validate(req.body);
  if (error) {
    return res.status(400).send(error.details[0].message);
```

```
  }
  next();
};
```

module.exports = validate;
```

This middleware checks if the incoming request body adheres to the specified schema. If validation fails, it returns a 400 status with an error message.

## 2. Protecting Routes with JWT Authentication

Authentication using JWT ensures that only authenticated users can access certain routes.

### Middleware for Authentication:

```js
const jwt = require('jsonwebtoken');

const auth = (req, res, next) => {
  const token = req.header('Authorization').replace('Bearer ', '');
  if (!token) {
    return res.status(401).send('Access denied. No token provided.');
  }
```
```

```js
  try {
    const decoded = jwt.verify(token, 'secretkey');
    req.user = decoded;
    next();
  } catch (error) {
    res.status(400).send('Invalid token.');
  }
};

module.exports = auth;
```

This middleware extracts the token from the Authorization header, verifies it, and attaches the decoded user information to the request object. If the token is missing or invalid, it denies access.

3. Role-Based Authorization

To enhance security, role-based access control ensures that users can only access resources they are permitted to.

Role Authorization Middleware:

```js
const Role = require('../models/Role');

const roleAuthorization = (requiredRole) => {
  return async (req, res, next) => {
```

```
  const { username } = req.user;
  const userRole = await Role.getUserRole(username);

  if (userRole !== requiredRole) {
    return res.status(403).send('Access denied. Insufficient permissions.');
  }
  next();
};

module.exports = roleAuthorization;
```

This middleware fetches the user's role from the database and checks if it matches the required role for accessing a particular route.

4. Database Interaction and Sanitization

Properly interacting with databases and ensuring input sanitization is crucial in preventing injection attacks. Let's explore how to handle these for both DynamoDB and PostgreSQL.

Sanitizing Inputs in PostgreSQL Queries:

```js
const pool = require('../database');
```

```js
class Role {
  static async getUserRole(username) {
    const sanitizedUsername = pool.escape(username);
    const result = await pool.query('SELECT role FROM user_roles WHERE username = $1', [sanitizedUsername]);
    return result.rows[0]?.role || null;
  }
}

module.exports = Role;
```

Here, using parameterized queries and escaping inputs helps in preventing SQL injection attacks.

- **Sanitizing Inputs in DynamoDB Operations:** DynamoDB inherently prevents injection attacks through its API design, as it doesn't execute raw queries. However, validating and sanitizing inputs before storing them is crucial.

Creating User with Sanitization:

```js
const dynamodb = require('../dynamodb');
const bcrypt = require('bcryptjs');
const { v4: uuidv4 } = require('uuid');

const USERS_TABLE = 'Users';
```

```
class User {
  static async create({ username, password }) {
    const sanitizedUsername = username.replace(/[^a-zA-Z0-9]/g, '');
    const hashedPassword = await bcrypt.hash(password, 10);

    const params = {
      TableName: USERS_TABLE,
      Item: {
        userId: uuidv4(),
        username: sanitizedUsername,
        password: hashedPassword,
      },
    };

    await dynamodb.put(params).promise();
  }

  static async findByUsername(username) {
    const sanitizedUsername = username.replace(/[^a-zA-Z0-9]/g, '');
    const params = {
      TableName: USERS_TABLE,
      Key: { username: sanitizedUsername },
    };

    const result = await dynamodb.get(params).promise();
```

```
    return result.Item;
}

module.exports = User;
```

By sanitizing the username to remove any non-alphanumeric characters, we ensure the data stored and queried is clean.

Practical Usage and Testing

To demonstrate the effectiveness of our validation and sanitization, let's create some test cases and use tools like Postman or curl to simulate requests.

Test Cases

1. Registration with Invalid Data:

```sh
curl -X POST http://localhost:3000/auth/register -H "Content-Type: application/json" -d '{"username": "usr", "password": "short"}'
```

Expected Response: `400 Bad Request` with message indicating validation failure.

2. Successful Registration:

```sh
curl -X POST http://localhost:3000/auth/register -H "Content-Type: application/json" -d '{"username": "validUser", "password": "ValidPassword123"}'
```

Expected Response: `201 Created` with success message.

3. Login with Incorrect Password:

```sh
curl -X POST http://localhost:3000/auth/login -H "Content-Type: application/json" -d '{"username": "validUser", "password": "wrongPassword"}'
```

Expected Response: `400 Bad Request` with message indicating invalid username or password.

4. Successful Login:

```sh
curl -X POST http://localhost:3000/auth/login -H "Content-Type: application/json" -d '{"username": "validUser", "password": "ValidPassword123"}'
```

Expected Response: `200 OK` with JWT token.

5. Access Protected Route without Token:

```sh
curl -X GET http://localhost:3000/protected/profile
```

Expected Response: `401 Unauthorized` with message indicating no token provided.

6. Access Protected Route with Token:

```sh
TOKEN="your_jwt_token_here"
curl -X GET http://localhost:3000/protected/profile -H "Authorization: Bearer $TOKEN"
```

Expected Response: `200 OK` with welcome message.

In this comprehensive guide, we have implemented robust data validation and sanitization techniques in a RESTful API using DynamoDB and PostgreSQL. By leveraging Joi for validation, express-validator for sanitization, and secure database interactions, we have built a resilient API that protects against malicious data injection attacks.

Key Takeaways:

1. Validation: Ensuring that input data conforms to expected formats and types.

2. Sanitization: Cleaning data to remove or escape harmful elements.

3. Authentication: Using JWT for secure user authentication.

4. Authorization: Implementing role-based access control to safeguard resources.

5. Database Security: Using parameterized queries and escaping inputs to prevent injection attacks.

By integrating these practices into your development workflow, you can enhance the security and reliability of your web applications, protecting them from common and sophisticated attacks.

Securing Communication Channels: Utilizing Encryption for Secure Data Transfer

In an era where data breaches and cyber threats are increasingly prevalent, securing communication channels has become a critical priority for developers and organizations. This document explores how to leverage encryption to secure data transfer within

RESTful APIs, specifically focusing on applications using DynamoDB and PostgreSQL. We'll delve into practical code examples and best practices for implementing encryption to ensure that data remains secure both in transit and at rest.

Introduction to Encryption

Encryption is the process of converting plain text into an unreadable format (cipher text) using a cryptographic algorithm and a key. The primary purpose of encryption is to protect the confidentiality and integrity of data. Encryption can be classified into two types: symmetric and asymmetric. Symmetric encryption uses the same key for both encryption and decryption, while asymmetric encryption uses a pair of keys (public and private keys).

Why Encryption is Essential for Secure Data Transfer

1. Confidentiality: Encryption ensures that only authorized parties can read the data.

2. Integrity: Encryption helps to verify that the data has not been altered during transmission.

3. Authentication: Encryption can verify the identity of the parties involved in the communication.

4. Compliance: Many regulations and standards require encryption to protect sensitive data.

RESTful API Overview

RESTful APIs are designed to enable communication between different systems over the HTTP/HTTPS protocol. They use standard HTTP methods such as GET, POST, PUT, and DELETE to perform CRUD (Create, Read, Update, Delete) operations. Ensuring the secure transfer of data via these APIs is crucial, especially when dealing with sensitive information.

Implementing Encryption in RESTful APIs

When building RESTful APIs, encryption can be applied both at the transport layer (using HTTPS) and at the application layer (encrypting the data itself).

Transport Layer Security (TLS)

Transport Layer Security (TLS) is a widely used protocol that ensures privacy between communicating applications and their users on the internet. To secure a

RESTful API, it is essential to use HTTPS, which is HTTP over TLS.

Application Layer Encryption

In addition to HTTPS, encrypting the data before it is transmitted over the network provides an extra layer of security. This is particularly important when dealing with highly sensitive data.

Setting Up the Environment

Before diving into encryption implementation, let's set up a basic environment with a RESTful API using Flask (a Python web framework), DynamoDB (a NoSQL database), and PostgreSQL (a relational database).

Flask Installation

First, install Flask using pip:
```bash
pip install Flask
```

DynamoDB Setup

We will use AWS SDK for Python (Boto3) to interact with DynamoDB. Install Boto3:

```bash
pip install boto3
```

PostgreSQL Setup

Install the necessary package to interact with PostgreSQL:
```bash
pip install psycopg2
```

Creating a Simple RESTful API

Let's create a simple RESTful API with endpoints to interact with DynamoDB and PostgreSQL.

API Structure

```
app/
├── app.py
├── dynamodb_handler.py
├── postgresql_handler.py
└── requirements.txt
```

app.py

This file will define the main Flask application.

```python
from flask import Flask, request, jsonify
from dynamodb_handler import DynamoDBHandler
from postgresql_handler import PostgreSQLHandler

app = Flask(__name__)
dynamo_handler = DynamoDBHandler()
postgres_handler = PostgreSQLHandler()

@app.route('/dynamodb', methods=['POST'])
def add_to_dynamodb():
    data = request.get_json()
    response = dynamo_handler.add_item(data)
    return jsonify(response)

@app.route('/postgresql', methods=['POST'])
def add_to_postgresql():
    data = request.get_json()
    response = postgres_handler.add_item(data)
    return jsonify(response)

if __name__ == '__main__':
    app.run(debug=True)
```

dynamodb_handler.py

This file will handle interactions with DynamoDB.

```python
import boto3
from botocore.exceptions import ClientError
import os
import json

class DynamoDBHandler:
    def __init__(self):
        self.dynamodb = boto3.resource('dynamodb', region_name='us-west-2')
        self.table = self.dynamodb.Table('YourDynamoDBTableName')

    def add_item(self, item):
        try:
            self.table.put_item(Item=item)
            return {"message": "Item added successfully"}
        except ClientError as e:
            return {"error": str(e)}
```

postgresql_handler.py

This file will handle interactions with PostgreSQL.

```python
import psycopg2
from psycopg2 import sql

class PostgreSQLHandler:
    def __init__(self):
        self.conn = psycopg2.connect(
            dbname="your_db_name",
            user="your_db_user",
            password="your_db_password",
            host="your_db_host",
            port="your_db_port"
        )
        self.cur = self.conn.cursor()

    def add_item(self, item):
        try:
            query = sql.SQL("INSERT INTO your_table (column1, column2) VALUES (%s, %s)")
            self.cur.execute(query, (item['column1'], item['column2']))
            self.conn.commit()
            return {"message": "Item added successfully"}
        except Exception as e:
            return {"error": str(e)}
```

Implementing Encryption

To implement encryption, we will use the `cryptography` library in Python. Install the library using pip:

```bash
pip install cryptography
```

Encrypting Data Before Storing in DynamoDB

We will encrypt the data before sending it to DynamoDB.

```python
from cryptography.fernet import Fernet

class DynamoDBHandler:
    def __init__(self):
        self.dynamodb = boto3.resource('dynamodb', region_name='us-west-2')
        self.table = self.dynamodb.Table('YourDynamoDBTableName')
        self.key = Fernet.generate_key()
        self.cipher_suite = Fernet(self.key)

    def add_item(self, item):
        try:
```

```
        for key in item:
            item[key] = self.cipher_suite.encrypt(item[key].encode()).decode()
        self.table.put_item(Item=item)
        return {"message": "Item added successfully", "key": self.key.decode()}
    except ClientError as e:
        return {"error": str(e)}
```

Decrypting Data Retrieved from DynamoDB

```python
class DynamoDBHandler:
    def __init__(self):
        self.dynamodb = boto3.resource('dynamodb', region_name='us-west-2')
        self.table = self.dynamodb.Table('YourDynamoDBTableName')

    def get_item(self, key, encryption_key):
        try:
            response = self.table.get_item(Key=key)
            item = response.get('Item')
            if item:
                cipher_suite = Fernet(encryption_key.encode())
                for k in item:
```

```
        item[k] = cipher_suite.decrypt(item[k].encode()).decode()
    return item
except ClientError as e:
    return {"error": str(e)}
```

Encrypting Data Before Storing in PostgreSQL

```python
class PostgreSQLHandler:
    def __init__(self):
        self.conn = psycopg2.connect(
            dbname="your_db_name",
            user="your_db_user",
            password="your_db_password",
            host="your_db_host",
            port="your_db_port"
        )
        self.cur = self.conn.cursor()
        self.key = Fernet.generate_key()
        self.cipher_suite = Fernet(self.key)

    def add_item(self, item):
        try:
            encrypted_item = {k: self.cipher_suite.encrypt(v.encode()).decode() for k, v in item.items()}
```

```
            query = sql.SQL("INSERT INTO your_table (column1, column2) VALUES (%s, %s)")
            self.cur.execute(query, (encrypted_item['column1'], encrypted_item['column2']))
            self.conn.commit()
            return {"message": "Item added successfully", "key": self.key.decode()}
        except Exception as e:
            return {"error": str(e)}
```

Decrypting Data Retrieved from PostgreSQL

```python
class PostgreSQLHandler:
    def __init__(self):
        self.conn = psycopg2.connect(
            dbname="your_db_name",
            user="your_db_user",
            password="your_db_password",
            host="your_db_host",
            port="your_db_port"
        )
        self.cur = self.conn.cursor()

    def get_item(self, item_id, encryption_key):
        try:
```

```
        query = sql.SQL("SELECT column1, column2 FROM your_table WHERE id = %s")
        self.cur.execute(query, (item_id,))
        result = self.cur.fetchone()
        if result:
            cipher_suite = Fernet(encryption_key.encode())
            decrypted_item = {k: cipher_suite.decrypt(v.encode()).decode() for k, v in zip(['column1', 'column2'], result)}
            return decrypted_item
        return None
    except Exception as e:
        return {"error": str(e)}
```
```

## Secure Data Transfer with HTTPS

To secure the data transfer, ensure that your Flask application uses HTTPS. This typically involves configuring your web server (e.g., Nginx or Apache) to use SSL/TLS certificates.

## Self-signed Certificates (For Testing)

You can generate self-signed certificates for testing purposes:
```

```bash
openssl req -x509 -newkey rsa:4096 -keyout key.pem -out cert.pem -days 365
```

Update your Flask application to use these certificates:

```python
if __name__ == '__main__':
    app.run(ssl_context=('cert.pem', 'key.pem'), debug=True)
```

This configuration will enable HTTPS on your local Flask server using the self-signed certificates.

Putting It All Together

Now that we have discussed the implementation of encryption for securing data both in transit and at rest, let's summarize and illustrate how these components come together to form a secure RESTful API.

Complete Flask Application with Encryption

Here's the complete example including encryption and HTTPS configuration.

app.py

```python
from flask import Flask, request, jsonify
from dynamodb_handler import DynamoDBHandler
from postgresql_handler import PostgreSQLHandler

app = Flask(__name__)
dynamo_handler = DynamoDBHandler()
postgres_handler = PostgreSQLHandler()

@app.route('/dynamodb', methods=['POST'])
def add_to_dynamodb():
    data = request.get_json()
    response = dynamo_handler.add_item(data)
    return jsonify(response)

@app.route('/dynamodb/<string:key>', methods=['GET'])
def get_from_dynamodb(key):
    encryption_key = request.headers.get('Encryption-Key')
    if not encryption_key:
        return jsonify({"error": "Encryption key is required"}), 400
    response = dynamo_handler.get_item({"PrimaryKey": key}, encryption_key)
    return jsonify(response)
```

```python
@app.route('/postgresql', methods=['POST'])
def add_to_postgresql():
    data = request.get_json()
    response = postgres_handler.add_item(data)
    return jsonify(response)

@app.route('/postgresql/<int:item_id>', methods=['GET'])
def get_from_postgresql(item_id):
    encryption_key = request.headers.get('Encryption-Key')
    if not encryption_key:
        return jsonify({"error": "Encryption key is required"}), 400
    response = postgres_handler.get_item(item_id, encryption_key)
    return jsonify(response)

if __name__ == '__main__':
    app.run(ssl_context=('cert.pem', 'key.pem'), debug=True)
```

dynamodb_handler.py

```python
import boto3
```

```python
from botocore.exceptions import ClientError
from cryptography.fernet import Fernet

class DynamoDBHandler:
    def __init__(self):
        self.dynamodb = boto3.resource('dynamodb', region_name='us-west-2')
        self.table = self.dynamodb.Table('YourDynamoDBTableName')
        self.key = Fernet.generate_key()
        self.cipher_suite = Fernet(self.key)

    def add_item(self, item):
        try:
            for key in item:
                item[key] = self.cipher_suite.encrypt(item[key].encode()).decode()
            self.table.put_item(Item=item)
            return {"message": "Item added successfully", "key": self.key.decode()}
        except ClientError as e:
            return {"error": str(e)}

    def get_item(self, key, encryption_key):
        try:
            response = self.table.get_item(Key=key)
            item = response.get('Item')
            if item:
```

```python
        cipher_suite = Fernet(encryption_key.encode())
        for k in item:
            item[k] = cipher_suite.decrypt(item[k].encode()).decode()
        return item
    except ClientError as e:
        return {"error": str(e)}
```

postgresql_handler.py

```python
import psycopg2
from psycopg2 import sql
from cryptography.fernet import Fernet

class PostgreSQLHandler:
    def __init__(self):
        self.conn = psycopg2.connect(
            dbname="your_db_name",
            user="your_db_user",
            password="your_db_password",
            host="your_db_host",
            port="your_db_port"
        )
        self.cur = self.conn.cursor()
        self.key = Fernet.generate_key()
```

```python
        self.cipher_suite = Fernet(self.key)

    def add_item(self, item):
        try:
            encrypted_item = {k: self.cipher_suite.encrypt(v.encode()).decode() for k, v in item.items()}
            query = sql.SQL("INSERT INTO your_table (column1, column2) VALUES (%s, %s)")
            self.cur.execute(query, (encrypted_item['column1'], encrypted_item['column2']))
            self.conn.commit()
            return {"message": "Item added successfully", "key": self.key.decode()}
        except Exception as e:
            return {"error": str(e)}

    def get_item(self, item_id, encryption_key):
        try:
            query = sql.SQL("SELECT column1, column2 FROM your_table WHERE id = %s")
            self.cur.execute(query, (item_id,))
            result = self.cur.fetchone()
            if result:
                cipher_suite = Fernet(encryption_key.encode())
```

```
            decrypted_item = {k:
cipher_suite.decrypt(v.encode()).decode() for k, v in
zip(['column1', 'column2'], result)}
            return decrypted_item
        return None
    except Exception as e:
        return {"error": str(e)}
```

Securing communication channels is imperative in today's digital landscape. By utilizing encryption, developers can significantly enhance the security of data transfers in RESTful APIs. This guide has demonstrated how to implement both transport layer security with HTTPS and application layer encryption using the `cryptography` library for data storage in DynamoDB and PostgreSQL.

The approach ensures that sensitive information remains confidential, maintains its integrity, and adheres to regulatory compliance. The examples provided serve as a foundation, which can be further expanded based on specific security requirements and use cases. Always remember to follow best practices for key management and keep your security libraries and protocols up to date to protect against emerging threats.

Monitoring and Logging: Keeping Track of API Activity and Identifying Potential Issues

Monitoring and logging are essential aspects of managing and maintaining a robust and efficient API. They help track the activity, performance, and health of an API, enabling developers to identify and troubleshoot potential issues quickly. This article explores techniques for monitoring and logging API activity, particularly focusing on RESTful APIs using DynamoDB and PostgreSQL. We'll cover best practices, provide code examples, and discuss tools to effectively implement monitoring and logging in your APIs.

Why Monitoring and Logging Are Important

1. Performance Tracking: Helps identify performance bottlenecks.

2. Error Detection: Quickly spot and diagnose errors.

3. Security Monitoring: Detect suspicious activities and potential security breaches.

4. Usage Analysis: Understand how your API is used and by whom.

5. Compliance: Ensure compliance with data protection regulations.

Monitoring API Activity

Metrics to Monitor

1. Request Metrics: Total number of requests, request rates, etc.

2. Latency Metrics: Response times, round-trip times, etc.

3. Error Metrics: Error rates, types of errors, etc.

4. Resource Metrics: CPU, memory usage, database query performance, etc.

Tools for Monitoring

1. AWS CloudWatch: For monitoring AWS resources like DynamoDB.

2. Prometheus: Open-source monitoring system with a dimensional data model.

3. Grafana: For visualization of Prometheus metrics.

4. New Relic: Comprehensive monitoring platform.

5. PostgreSQL Metrics Collection: Extensions like pg_stat_statements for query performance.

Implementing Monitoring

Using AWS CloudWatch with DynamoDB

AWS CloudWatch is a powerful tool for monitoring AWS resources, including DynamoDB. Here's how you can set it up:

1. Enable CloudWatch for DynamoDB:

```python
import boto3

client = boto3.client('dynamodb')
response = client.update_table(
    TableName='YourTableName',
    ProvisionedThroughput={
        'ReadCapacityUnits': 5,
        'WriteCapacityUnits': 5
    }
```

2. Create a CloudWatch Dashboard:

```python
import boto3

cloudwatch = boto3.client('cloudwatch')

response = cloudwatch.put_dashboard(
    DashboardName='DynamoDBDashboard',
    DashboardBody='''{
      "widgets": [
        {
          "type": "metric",
          "x": 0,
          "y": 0,
          "width": 6,
          "height": 6,
          "properties": {
            "metrics": [
              [ "AWS/DynamoDB", "ReadThrottleEvents", "TableName", "YourTableName" ]
            ],
            "period": 300,
            "stat": "Sum",
            "region": "us-west-2",
            "title": "Read Throttle Events"
          }
        }
'''
```

Using Prometheus and Grafana for PostgreSQL

Prometheus can scrape metrics from PostgreSQL, and Grafana can visualize them. Here's a basic setup:

1. Install PostgreSQL Exporter:

```bash
docker run --name postgres-exporter \
  -e DATA_SOURCE_NAME="postgresql://user:password@hostname:port/dbname?sslmode=disable" \
  quay.io/prometheuscommunity/postgres-exporter
```

2. Configure Prometheus:

```yaml
global:
  scrape_interval: 15s

scrape_configs:
  - job_name: 'postgres'
    static_configs:
      - targets: ['localhost:9187']
```

3. Visualize with Grafana:

- Add Prometheus as a data source in Grafana.

- Create dashboards using PostgreSQL metrics from Prometheus.

Logging API Activity

What to Log

1. Request Data: HTTP method, endpoint, headers, parameters, payload, etc.

2. Response Data: Status code, response time, response payload, etc.

3. Error Logs: Stack traces, error messages, etc.

4. Access Logs: User IDs, IP addresses, authentication details, etc.

Tools for Logging

1. AWS CloudWatch Logs: For logging DynamoDB and other AWS service logs.

2. ELK Stack (Elasticsearch, Logstash, Kibana): For comprehensive log management.

3. Fluentd: Unified logging layer.

4. Winston: Logging library for Node.js applications.

5. Logback: Logging framework for Java applications.

Implementing Logging

Using AWS CloudWatch Logs for DynamoDB

To enable logging for DynamoDB, you can stream the DynamoDB table changes to CloudWatch Logs using AWS Lambda.

1. Create a Lambda Function:

```python
import boto3
import json

def lambda_handler(event, context):
    logs_client = boto3.client('logs')
    log_group_name = 'DynamoDBTableLogs'
    log_stream_name = 'TableStream'
```

```
for record in event['Records']:
    if record['eventName'] == 'INSERT':
        new_image = record['dynamodb']['NewImage']
        logs_client.put_log_events(
            logGroupName=log_group_name,
            logStreamName=log_stream_name,
            logEvents=[
                {
                    'timestamp': int(record['dynamodb']['ApproximateCreationDateTime'] * 1000),
                    'message': json.dumps(new_image)
                }
```
```

## 2. Set up DynamoDB Stream:

```python
dynamodb = boto3.client('dynamodb')

response = dynamodb.update_table(
    TableName='YourTableName',
    StreamSpecification={
        'StreamEnabled': True,
        'StreamViewType': 'NEW_IMAGE'
    }
```
```

3. Connect Lambda to DynamoDB Stream: Create an Event Source Mapping in Lambda linking your DynamoDB stream to the Lambda function.

Using ELK Stack for API Logs

1. Install and Configure Logstash:

```yaml
input {
  http {
    port => 5044
  }
}
filter {
  json {
    source => "message"
  }
}
output {
  elasticsearch {
    hosts => ["localhost:9200"]
    index => "api-logs-%{+YYYY.MM.dd}"
  }
}
```

2. Send Logs to Logstash from Your API:

```python
```

```python
import logging
import requests

logger = logging.getLogger('api_logger')
logger.setLevel(logging.INFO)

def log_request(request, response):
    log_data = {
        'method': request.method,
        'url': request.url,
        'status_code': response.status_code,
        'response_time': response.elapsed.total_seconds(),
        'request_body': request.json,
        'response_body': response.json()
    }
    requests.post('http://localhost:5044', json=log_data)

# Example usage in an API endpoint
from flask import Flask, request

app = Flask(__name__)

@app.route('/data', methods=['POST'])
def data():
    response = some_database_operation(request.json)
    log_request(request, response)
    return response
```

```
if __name__ == '__main__':
    app.run(debug=True)
```
```

### 3. Visualize Logs with Kibana:

- Set up Kibana to connect to Elasticsearch.

- Create dashboards and visualizations for your API logs.

## Identifying Potential Issues

## Common API Issues

**1. Performance Degradation:** Slow response times or increased latency.

**2. High Error Rates:** Increased HTTP 4xx/5xx errors.

**3. Resource Constraints:** High CPU or memory usage.

**4. Security Threats:** Unusual access patterns or suspicious activities.

**5. Data Consistency Issues:** Discrepancies in data stored in DynamoDB or PostgreSQL.
```

Using Logs and Metrics to Identify Issues

1. Performance Bottlenecks:

- **Metrics**: Monitor latency metrics.

- **Logs**: Analyze response times and identify slow endpoints.

- **Example**: Using CloudWatch or Prometheus to monitor response times.

2. Error Analysis:

- **Metrics**: Track error rates.

- **Logs**: Analyze error logs and stack traces.

- **Example**: Using ELK Stack to filter and search for error logs.

3. Resource Utilization:

- **Metrics**: Monitor CPU and memory usage.

- **Logs**: Correlate high usage periods with specific requests.

- **Example**: Using Grafana to visualize Prometheus metrics.

4. **Security Monitoring:**

- **Metrics**: Track unusual access patterns.
- **Logs**: Analyze access logs for suspicious activities.
- **Example**: Using AWS CloudWatch to set alarms on unusual login attempts.

5. **Data Consistency:**

- **Metrics**: Monitor data integrity checks.
- **Logs**: Log data inconsistencies and anomalies.
- **Example**: Custom Lambda function to log data discrepancies in DynamoDB streams.

Effective monitoring and logging are critical for maintaining the health and performance of your APIs. By leveraging tools like AWS CloudWatch, Prometheus, Grafana, and the ELK Stack, you can gain valuable insights into your API's activity, detect and resolve issues promptly, and ensure a smooth and secure user experience. Integrating these practices into your development workflow will lead to more reliable and resilient APIs, ultimately enhancing user satisfaction and reducing downtime.

Best Practices for Monitoring and Logging

1. Consistent and Comprehensive Logging

Ensure that your logging strategy is consistent across all components of your API. Log requests and responses uniformly, capturing sufficient detail without overwhelming your logging system. Include timestamps, unique request IDs, and relevant contextual information to facilitate debugging and analysis.

2. Use Structured Logging

Adopt structured logging formats, such as JSON, to enable easier parsing and analysis of logs. Structured logs make it simpler to filter and search for specific events, correlate related logs, and extract meaningful insights using log management tools.

3. Implement Centralized Logging

Centralize logs from all parts of your system into a single location, such as an ELK stack or AWS

CloudWatch Logs. This consolidation helps streamline log analysis, reduces the complexity of accessing logs from different sources, and facilitates comprehensive monitoring of your system's health.

4. Monitor Key Metrics Proactively

Identify and monitor key performance indicators (KPIs) for your API. These might include request rates, latency, error rates, and resource utilization metrics. Set up alerts for anomalies or thresholds that indicate potential issues, allowing your team to respond swiftly.

5. Automate and Integrate Monitoring Tools

Automate the setup and configuration of your monitoring and logging tools to ensure consistency and reduce manual errors. Integrate these tools with your CI/CD pipeline to automatically deploy updates and configuration changes, keeping your monitoring setup up-to-date with the latest application changes.

6. Regularly Review and Refine Monitoring Strategies

Regularly review your monitoring and logging strategies to ensure they remain effective as your API evolves. Update your metrics, logs, and alerts based on new insights, user feedback, and changes in your API's architecture and usage patterns.

7. Ensure Security and Compliance

Ensure that your logging practices comply with relevant data protection and privacy regulations. Mask or exclude sensitive data from logs, and implement access controls to protect your logs from unauthorized access. Use encryption for logs both in transit and at rest.

8. Use Visualization Tools

Leverage visualization tools like Grafana and Kibana to create intuitive dashboards that provide real-time insights into your API's performance and health. Visualizations can help quickly identify trends, anomalies, and potential issues, facilitating more effective monitoring.

Example: Building a Monitoring and Logging Setup

Let's walk through an example of setting up monitoring and logging for a RESTful API using DynamoDB and PostgreSQL.

Step 1: Setting Up CloudWatch for DynamoDB

First, enable AWS CloudWatch for your DynamoDB table and create a dashboard to monitor key metrics.

```python
import boto3

# Enable CloudWatch for DynamoDB
client = boto3.client('dynamodb')
response = client.update_table(
    TableName='YourTableName',
    ProvisionedThroughput={
        'ReadCapacityUnits': 5,
        'WriteCapacityUnits': 5
    }
# Create CloudWatch Dashboard
cloudwatch = boto3.client('cloudwatch')

dashboard_body = '''
{
    "widgets": [
        {
            "type": "metric",
            "x": 0,
            "y": 0,
            "width": 6,
            "height": 6,
            "properties": {
                "metrics": [
```

```
                [ "AWS/DynamoDB",
"ReadThrottleEvents", "TableName", "YourTableName"
]
          ],
          "period": 300,
          "stat": "Sum",
          "region": "us-west-2",
          "title": "Read Throttle Events"
        }
  '''
response = cloudwatch.put_dashboard(
    DashboardName='DynamoDBDashboard',
    DashboardBody=dashboard_body
)
```

Step 2: Setting Up Prometheus and Grafana for PostgreSQL

Install and configure Prometheus to scrape metrics from PostgreSQL, and set up Grafana for visualization.

1. Install PostgreSQL Exporter:

```bash
docker run --name postgres-exporter \
```

```
  -e DATA_SOURCE_NAME="postgresql://user:password@hostname:port/dbname?sslmode=disable" \
  quay.io/prometheuscommunity/postgres-exporter
```

2. Configure Prometheus:

Create a `prometheus.yml` configuration file:

```yaml
global:
  scrape_interval: 15s

scrape_configs:
  - job_name: 'postgres'
    static_configs:
      - targets: ['localhost:9187']
```

3. Run Prometheus:

```bash
docker run -d --name prometheus \
  -v /path/to/prometheus.yml:/etc/prometheus/prometheus.yml \
  -p 9090:9090 \
```

      prom/prometheus
```

## 4. Set Up Grafana:

- Install Grafana and add Prometheus as a data source.

- Create dashboards to visualize PostgreSQL metrics.

## Step 3: Implementing API Logging with ELK Stack

## 1. Install and Configure Logstash:

Create a Logstash configuration file (`logstash.conf`):

```yaml
input {
  http {
    port => 5044
  }
filter {
  json {
    source => "message"
  }
output {
  elasticsearch {
```
```

```
    hosts => ["localhost:9200"]
    index => "api-logs-%{+YYYY.MM.dd}"
  }
}
```

2. Send Logs to Logstash from Your API:

Integrate logging into your API endpoints:

```python
import logging
import requests
from flask import Flask, request, jsonify

logger = logging.getLogger('api_logger')
logger.setLevel(logging.INFO)

app = Flask(__name__)

def log_request(request, response):
    log_data = {
        'method': request.method,
        'url': request.url,
        'status_code': response.status_code,
        'response_time': response.elapsed.total_seconds(),
        'request_body': request.json,
        'response_body': response.json()
    }
```

```
requests.post('http://localhost:5044', json=log_data)

@app.route('/data', methods=['POST'])
def data():
    # Simulate a database operation
    response = jsonify({'message': 'Data received'})
    response.status_code = 200
    log_request(request, response)
    return response

if __name__ == '__main__':
    app.run(debug=True)
```

3. Visualize Logs with Kibana:

- Install Kibana and configure it to connect to Elasticsearch.

- Create visualizations and dashboards for your API logs.

Monitoring and logging are critical components of a robust and reliable API infrastructure. By leveraging tools like AWS CloudWatch, Prometheus, Grafana, and the ELK Stack, you can gain deep insights into your API's performance, quickly identify and resolve issues, and ensure a high-quality experience for your users.

Implementing the best practices and examples outlined in this article will help you build a resilient and well-monitored API system using DynamoDB and PostgreSQL.

Chapter 9

Choosing the Right Deployment Environment: Cloud or On-Premises Considerations

When developing a RESTful API, one of the critical decisions developers must make is whether to deploy the application on a cloud platform or on-premises infrastructure. This decision impacts various aspects such as scalability, cost, performance, and maintenance. In this article, we will explore these considerations by building a RESTful API using DynamoDB and PostgreSQL, comparing cloud and on-premises deployment environments.

Overview of RESTful API, DynamoDB, and PostgreSQL

A RESTful API is a web service that follows the principles of Representational State Transfer (REST). It uses HTTP requests to perform CRUD (Create, Read, Update, Delete) operations on resources identified by URIs. This API architecture is stateless, meaning each request from a client to a server must contain all the information the server needs to fulfill the request.

DynamoDB is a fully managed NoSQL database service provided by Amazon Web Services (AWS). It offers high availability, scalability, and performance, making it suitable for applications that require a flexible schema and handle large amounts of unstructured data.

PostgreSQL is an open-source relational database management system (RDBMS) known for its robustness, feature set, and compliance with SQL standards. It is ideal for applications that need ACID (Atomicity, Consistency, Isolation, Durability) properties and complex querying capabilities.

Building a RESTful API

We will demonstrate the basic implementation of a RESTful API using both DynamoDB and PostgreSQL. Below is a simplified example of a Python Flask application with endpoints to create and retrieve data from these databases.

Setting Up the Project

```bash
$ mkdir rest_api
$ cd rest_api
$ python3 -m venv venv
$ source venv/bin/activate
```

```
$ pip install flask boto3 psycopg2-binary
```

Basic Flask Application Structure

```python
# app.py
from flask import Flask, request, jsonify
import boto3
import psycopg2

app = Flask(__name__)

# DynamoDB setup
dynamodb = boto3.resource('dynamodb', region_name='us-east-1')
table = dynamodb.Table('Items')

# PostgreSQL setup
conn = psycopg2.connect(
    dbname="your_db",
    user="your_user",
    password="your_password",
    host="your_host",
    port="your_port"
)
cursor = conn.cursor()
```

```python
# Create item in DynamoDB
@app.route('/dynamodb/item', methods=['POST'])
def create_dynamodb_item():
    item = request.json
    table.put_item(Item=item)
    return jsonify({'message': 'Item created in DynamoDB'}), 201

# Retrieve item from DynamoDB
@app.route('/dynamodb/item/<string:item_id>', methods=['GET'])
def get_dynamodb_item(item_id):
    response = table.get_item(Key={'item_id': item_id})
    return jsonify(response['Item'])

# Create item in PostgreSQL
@app.route('/postgresql/item', methods=['POST'])
def create_postgresql_item():
    item = request.json
    cursor.execute(
        "INSERT INTO items (id, name, value) VALUES (%s, %s, %s)",
        (item['id'], item['name'], item['value'])
    )
    conn.commit()
    return jsonify({'message': 'Item created in PostgreSQL'}), 201
```

```
# Retrieve item from PostgreSQL
@app.route('/postgresql/item/<int:item_id>',
methods=['GET'])
def get_postgresql_item(item_id):
    cursor.execute("SELECT * FROM items WHERE id = %s", (item_id,))
    item = cursor.fetchone()
    return jsonify({'id': item[0], 'name': item[1], 'value': item[2]})

if __name__ == '__main__':
    app.run(debug=True)
```
```

## Cloud vs. On-Premises: Key Considerations

**1. Scalability**

**Cloud**:

- **Automatic Scaling:** Cloud services like AWS offer auto-scaling features, which automatically adjust resources to match the load. For instance, DynamoDB can handle sudden traffic spikes seamlessly without manual intervention.

- **Global Reach:** Cloud platforms provide data centers around the globe, allowing applications to
```

serve users with minimal latency by deploying resources closer to end-users.

On-Premises:

- **Manual Scaling:** Scaling on-premises infrastructure typically requires purchasing and installing new hardware, which can be time-consuming and costly.

- **Limited by Physical Resources:** Scalability is constrained by the physical limitations of the infrastructure and the ability to manage and maintain it.

2. Cost

Cloud:

- **Pay-as-You-Go:** Cloud providers charge based on usage, which can be cost-effective for variable workloads. For example, DynamoDB charges based on read/write capacity and storage used.

- **Operational Expenditure (OPEX):** Costs are categorized as OPEX, with ongoing expenses based on consumption, reducing the need for significant upfront investment.

On-Premises:

- **Capital Expenditure (CAPEX):** Initial costs for purchasing hardware and setting up the infrastructure can be high. This model might be more suitable for predictable workloads and long-term usage.

- **Maintenance Costs:** Additional expenses for maintenance, upgrades, and power consumption must be considered.

3. Performance

Cloud:

- **Optimized Resources:** Cloud providers optimize their data centers for performance, offering high-speed networks, SSD storage, and advanced caching mechanisms.

- **Latency:** Performance can be affected by network latency, especially if the cloud data center is far from the end-user.

On-Premises:

- **Low Latency:** Locally hosted applications can offer lower latency, beneficial for use cases requiring real-time data processing.

- **Resource Control:** Full control over hardware specifications and performance tuning can optimize the system to meet specific application needs.

4. Security

Cloud:

- **Built-In Security:** Cloud providers offer robust security features, including encryption, firewalls, DDoS protection, and compliance with industry standards (e.g., GDPR, HIPAA).

- **Shared Responsibility Model:** While the provider ensures the infrastructure's security, users are responsible for securing their applications and data within the cloud.

On-Premises:

- **Full Control:** Organizations have complete control over security measures, physical access, and compliance policies.

- **Resource-Intensive:** Implementing and maintaining high-security standards requires dedicated resources and expertise.

5. Maintenance and Management

<u>Cloud</u>:

- **Managed Services:** Cloud platforms offer managed services (e.g., DynamoDB), reducing the need for administrative tasks like patching, backups, and monitoring.

- **Continuous Updates:** Providers continuously update their services with new features and performance improvements.

<u>On-Premises:</u>

- **In-House Management:** Requires a dedicated IT team for infrastructure management, updates, and troubleshooting.

- **Customization**: More flexibility to customize and optimize the environment according to specific requirements.

Use Case Comparison

To better understand the implications of deploying on the cloud versus on-premises, let's examine a use case for each database: DynamoDB and PostgreSQL.

DynamoDB in the Cloud

Scenario:

A startup needs to deploy a RESTful API for a mobile application that expects unpredictable traffic patterns and rapid growth.

Considerations:

- **Scalability**: DynamoDB's ability to auto-scale and handle high-throughput requests makes it ideal for this scenario.

- **Cost**: The pay-as-you-go model helps manage costs, especially during the early stages with variable traffic.

- **Management**: Using AWS's managed services reduces the overhead of database administration, allowing the startup to focus on application development.

Implementation:

Deploy the Flask application on AWS Lambda (serverless) with API Gateway, and use DynamoDB for data storage. This architecture ensures scalability, cost-efficiency, and minimal maintenance.

```python
# Lambda handler
def lambda_handler(event, context):
    app = Flask(__name__)
    return app(event, context)
```

PostgreSQL On-Premises

Scenario:

A financial institution needs to deploy a RESTful API for an internal application with stringent compliance and data sovereignty requirements.

Considerations:

- **Security**: Full control over security measures and compliance with regulatory requirements is critical.

- **Performance**: Low latency and high performance for real-time transactions are necessary.

- **Cost**: The institution has the resources to invest in and maintain the necessary infrastructure.

Implementation:

Deploy the Flask application on an on-premises server with PostgreSQL installed. This setup ensures compliance with regulatory standards and provides the necessary control over security and performance.

```bash
# PostgreSQL setup script
sudo apt-get update
sudo apt-get install postgresql postgresql-contrib
sudo -u postgres psql -c "CREATE DATABASE your_db;"
sudo -u postgres psql -c "CREATE USER your_user WITH PASSWORD 'your_password';"
sudo -u postgres psql -c "GRANT ALL PRIVILEGES ON DATABASE your_db TO your_user;"
```

Choosing between cloud and on-premises deployment for a RESTful API depends on various factors, including scalability, cost, performance, security, and maintenance.

- Cloud deployment services like DynamoDB are suitable for applications requiring high scalability, flexibility, and lower maintenance overhead.

- On-premises deployment PostgreSQL is ideal for scenarios needing stringent security, compliance, and performance control.

By understanding these considerations, developers can make informed decisions that align with their application's requirements and organizational goals.

Configuration for Deployment: Optimizing Your API for Production Usage

Deploying a RESTful API built with DynamoDB and PostgreSQL for production usage involves more than just writing code. It requires careful consideration of various configurations and optimizations to ensure performance, scalability, security, and maintainability. In this guide, we'll explore the essential configurations and optimizations needed to deploy a robust and efficient API.

1. Environment Configuration

DynamoDB:

```python
import boto3

# Initialize DynamoDB client
dynamodb = boto3.client('dynamodb')

# Create table if not exists
def create_dynamodb_table():
    try:
        dynamodb.create_table(
            TableName='Items',
            KeySchema=[
                {'AttributeName': 'id', 'KeyType': 'HASH'}
            ],
            AttributeDefinitions=[
                {'AttributeName': 'id', 'AttributeType': 'S'}
            ],
            ProvisionedThroughput={
                'ReadCapacityUnits': 5,
                'WriteCapacityUnits': 5
            }
        )
    except dynamodb.exceptions.ResourceInUseException:
```

```
    pass
```

PostgreSQL:

```python
import psycopg2

# Initialize PostgreSQL connection
conn = psycopg2.connect(
    dbname="your_db",
    user="your_user",
    password="your_password",
    host="your_host",
    port="your_port"
)
cursor = conn.cursor()

# Create table if not exists
def create_postgresql_table():
    cursor.execute(
        """
        CREATE TABLE IF NOT EXISTS items (
            id SERIAL PRIMARY KEY,
            name VARCHAR(255),
            value INTEGER
        )
        """
```

    conn.commit()
```

## 2. Performance Optimization

**DynamoDB**:

```python
# Batch operations for DynamoDB
def batch_get_items(keys):
    response = dynamodb.batch_get_item(
        RequestItems={
            'Items': {
                'Keys': keys
            }
        }

    return response['Responses']['Items']

def batch_write_items(items):
    with dynamodb.batch_writer() as batch:
        for item in items:
            batch.put_item(Item=item)
```

PostgreSQL:

```python
# Connection pooling for PostgreSQL
```
```

```python
from psycopg2 import pool

connection_pool = pool.SimpleConnectionPool(
    1,  # min connections
    10,  # max connections
    dbname="your_db",
    user="your_user",
    password="your_password",
    host="your_host",
    port="your_port"
)

# Execute query with connection pooling
def execute_query(query, params=None):
    connection = connection_pool.getconn()
    cursor = connection.cursor()
    cursor.execute(query, params)
    result = cursor.fetchall()
    cursor.close()
    connection_pool.putconn(connection)
    return result
```

3. Security Configuration

DynamoDB:

```python
```

```python
# IAM policies for DynamoDB
def create_iam_policy():
    iam = boto3.client('iam')
    policy_document = {
        "Version": "2012-10-17",
        "Statement": [{
            "Effect": "Allow",
            "Action": "dynamodb:*",
            "Resource": "*"
        }]
    }
    iam.create_policy(
        PolicyName='DynamoDBFullAccess',
        PolicyDocument=json.dumps(policy_document)
    )
```

PostgreSQL:

```python
# Secure connection for PostgreSQL
conn = psycopg2.connect(
    dbname="your_db",
    user="your_user",
    password="your_password",
    host="your_host",
    port="your_port",
    sslmode="require"
)
```

```

## 4. Deployment Configuration

**DynamoDB**:

```python
# Multi-region replication for DynamoDB
def enable_multi_region_replication():
    dynamodb.create_global_table(
        TableName='Items',
        ReplicationGroup=[
            {'RegionName': 'us-west-1'},
            {'RegionName': 'us-east-1'}
        ]
```

PostgreSQL:

```python
# High availability for PostgreSQL
def configure_high_availability():
    cursor.execute(
        "CREATE EXTENSION IF NOT EXISTS pgpool_recovery"
    )
    conn.commit()
```
```

Optimizing your API for production usage involves configuring and fine-tuning various aspects such as environment setup, performance optimization, security configuration, and deployment configuration. By following best practices and leveraging the capabilities of DynamoDB and PostgreSQL, you can deploy a robust and efficient API that meets the demands of modern applications while ensuring data integrity, security, and performance.

Monitoring and Maintaining Your API: Keeping Your Creation Running Smoothly

Monitoring and maintaining your RESTful API is essential for ensuring its reliability, performance, and availability. By implementing effective monitoring strategies and maintenance routines, you can identify and address issues proactively, minimize downtime, and optimize performance. In this guide, we'll explore how to monitor and maintain a RESTful API built with DynamoDB and PostgreSQL, along with code examples for implementation.

1. Monitoring Strategies

DynamoDB:

- **CloudWatch Metrics:** Monitor key metrics such as read/write capacity utilization, throttled requests, and latency using CloudWatch metrics. Set up alarms to notify you of any performance issues or capacity constraints.

```python
import boto3

# Initialize DynamoDB client
dynamodb = boto3.client('dynamodb')

# Get CloudWatch metrics for DynamoDB table
def get_dynamodb_metrics(table_name):
    response = dynamodb.describe_table(TableName=table_name)
    return response['Table']['TableArn']
```

PostgreSQL:

- **Query Performance Monitoring:** Monitor query performance metrics such as execution time, rows fetched, and index usage using PostgreSQL's built-in `pg_stat_statements` extension.

```python
```

```python
import psycopg2

# Initialize PostgreSQL connection
conn = psycopg2.connect(
    dbname="your_db",
    user="your_user",
    password="your_password",
    host="your_host",
    port="your_port"
)
cursor = conn.cursor()

# Get query performance metrics from pg_stat_statements
def get_query_performance_metrics():
    cursor.execute(
        """
        SELECT queryid, query, total_time, rows
        FROM pg_stat_statements
        ORDER BY total_time DESC
        LIMIT 10
        """
    )
    return cursor.fetchall()
```

2. Maintenance Routines

DynamoDB:

- **Auto Scaling Configuration:** Regularly review and adjust auto-scaling settings based on workload patterns and usage trends to ensure optimal resource utilization and performance.

```python
# Update DynamoDB auto-scaling settings
def update_auto_scaling_settings(table_name, read_capacity_units, write_capacity_units):
    dynamodb.update_table(
        TableName=table_name,
        ProvisionedThroughput={
            'ReadCapacityUnits': read_capacity_units,
            'WriteCapacityUnits': write_capacity_units
        }
```

PostgreSQL:

- **Vacuum and Analyze:** Schedule regular vacuum and analyze operations to reclaim disk space, update statistics, and optimize query performance.

```python
# Perform vacuum and analyze operations
```

```
def perform_vacuum_and_analyze():
    cursor.execute("VACUUM FULL ANALYZE")
    conn.commit()
```

3. Health Checks

DynamoDB:

- **Table Health Checks:** Periodically check the health of DynamoDB tables by monitoring throughput capacity, latency, and error rates.

```python
# Check DynamoDB table health
def check_dynamodb_table_health(table_name):
    response = dynamodb.describe_table(TableName=table_name)
    if response['Table']['TableStatus'] == 'ACTIVE':
        return True
    else:
        return False
```

PostgreSQL:

- **Database Health Checks:** Implement health checks to monitor PostgreSQL database availability, connectivity, and performance.

```python
# Check PostgreSQL database health
def check_postgresql_health():
    try:
        conn.ping()
        return True
    except psycopg2.Error as e:
        return False
```

4. Logging and Alerting

DynamoDB:

- **CloudWatch Logs:** Stream API logs to CloudWatch Logs for centralized logging and analysis. Set up metric filters and alarms to detect errors, throttling, and performance issues.

```python
# Log API requests to CloudWatch Logs
def log_to_cloudwatch_logs(event):
    # Log event details
    print(event)
```

```python
# Example usage in Flask app
@app.route('/api/resource', methods=['GET'])
def get_resource():
    log_to_cloudwatch_logs(request)
    # API logic
```

PostgreSQL:

- **Query Logging:** Enable query logging in PostgreSQL to capture SQL statements, execution plans, and performance statistics for analysis and troubleshooting.

```python
# Enable query logging in PostgreSQL
def enable_query_logging():
    cursor.execute("ALTER SYSTEM SET log_statement = 'all'")
    cursor.execute("ALTER SYSTEM SET log_min_duration_statement = 1000")
    conn.commit()
```

Monitoring and maintaining your RESTful API built with DynamoDB and PostgreSQL is crucial for ensuring its reliability, performance, and availability. By implementing effective monitoring strategies, maintenance routines, health checks, logging, and alerting mechanisms, you can proactively identify and address issues, minimize downtime, and optimize performance to keep your API running smoothly. With the code examples provided, you can easily integrate these monitoring and maintenance features into your API implementation for enhanced reliability and operational excellence.

Conclusion

In conclusion, building a RESTful API with DynamoDB and PostgreSQL offers a powerful combination of flexibility, scalability, and reliability. Throughout this guide, we've explored the process of creating, deploying, monitoring, and maintaining such an API, providing insights and code examples to help you navigate each step of the way.

DynamoDB, with its fully managed NoSQL database service, offers high availability, scalability, and performance, making it an excellent choice for applications that require flexibility and handle large amounts of unstructured data. On the other hand, PostgreSQL, an open-source relational database management system, provides robustness, compliance with SQL standards, and ACID properties, making it ideal for applications that demand data integrity and complex querying capabilities.

By leveraging the strengths of both databases, developers can build RESTful APIs that meet the demands of modern applications while ensuring reliability and performance. Whether deploying on the cloud or on-premises infrastructure, careful consideration of factors such as scalability, cost, security, and maintenance is essential to make informed decisions and optimize the API's performance.

Monitoring and maintaining the API is crucial for ensuring its smooth operation over time. Implementing effective monitoring strategies, maintenance routines, health checks, logging, and alerting mechanisms allows developers to proactively identify and address issues, minimize downtime, and optimize performance.

As technology evolves and user expectations continue to rise, the need for robust and efficient APIs becomes increasingly critical. By following best practices and leveraging the capabilities of DynamoDB and PostgreSQL, developers can build RESTful APIs that not only meet the current requirements but also adapt and scale to future needs.

In the ever-changing landscape of software development, building and maintaining a high-quality RESTful API is not just a one-time task but an ongoing process. With dedication, attention to detail, and a commitment to excellence, developers can create APIs that power innovative applications, drive business growth, and deliver exceptional user experiences.

Appendix

Glossary of Terms

RESTful API: A Representational State Transfer (REST) API is a web service that follows the principles of REST architecture. It uses standard HTTP methods (GET, POST, PUT, DELETE) to perform CRUD operations on resources identified by URIs.

DynamoDB: DynamoDB is a fully managed NoSQL database service provided by Amazon Web Services (AWS). It offers high availability, scalability, and performance, making it suitable for applications that require flexible schema and handle large amounts of unstructured data.

PostgreSQL: PostgreSQL is an open-source relational database management system (RDBMS) known for its robustness, feature set, and compliance with SQL standards. It is ideal for applications that need ACID (Atomicity, Consistency, Isolation, Durability) properties and complex querying capabilities.

NoSQL: NoSQL databases, such as DynamoDB, are non-relational databases that provide a flexible schema and are optimized for handling large volumes of unstructured or semi-structured data.

ACID: ACID stands for Atomicity, Consistency, Isolation, and Durability. It is a set of properties that ensure database transactions are processed reliably.

HTTP Methods: HTTP methods define the actions that can be performed on a resource. Common HTTP methods used in RESTful APIs include GET (retrieve data), POST (create data), PUT (update data), and DELETE (delete data).

CRUD Operations: CRUD stands for Create, Read, Update, and Delete. These are the basic operations performed on data in a database or API.

Cloud Deployment: Cloud deployment refers to hosting an application or service on a cloud platform, such as AWS, Microsoft Azure, or Google Cloud Platform. Cloud deployment offers benefits such as scalability, flexibility, and cost-effectiveness.

On-Premises Deployment: On-premises deployment refers to hosting an application or service on infrastructure located within an organization's own data center or premises, rather than on a cloud platform.

Auto Scaling: Auto scaling is a feature provided by cloud services that automatically adjusts resources (such as compute instances or database capacity) based on demand, ensuring optimal performance and cost efficiency.

High Availability: High availability refers to the ability of a system or service to remain operational and accessible even in the event of hardware failures, software bugs, or other disruptions.

Connection Pooling: Connection pooling is a technique used to manage a pool of reusable database connections, reducing the overhead of establishing new connections and improving performance.

Encryption at Rest: Encryption at rest refers to the practice of encrypting data stored in a database or on disk to protect it from unauthorized access in case of theft or physical compromise.

SSL/TLS Encryption: SSL (Secure Sockets Layer) and TLS (Transport Layer Security) are cryptographic protocols used to encrypt data transmitted over a network, ensuring confidentiality and integrity.

Health Checks: Health checks are periodic evaluations of a system or service to assess its operational status, connectivity, and performance.

Logging and Alerting: Logging involves capturing and storing detailed information about system events, errors, and user activities for analysis and troubleshooting. Alerting involves setting up notifications or alarms to alert administrators or developers about critical events or performance issues.

Common Libraries and Frameworks for Building APIs with DynamoDB and PostgreSQL

Building RESTful APIs with DynamoDB and PostgreSQL involves leveraging common libraries and frameworks to streamline development and ensure robustness. Let's delve into the essential tools and techniques for crafting APIs using these databases.

Introduction to DynamoDB and PostgreSQL:

DynamoDB is a fully managed NoSQL database service provided by AWS, offering seamless scalability, low latency, and high availability. On the other hand, PostgreSQL is a powerful open-source relational database known for its extensibility, reliability, and SQL compliance.

Setting Up the Environment:

Before diving into API development, ensure you have the necessary tools installed, such as Node.js, npm, and AWS SDK for JavaScript. Additionally, set up your DynamoDB and PostgreSQL instances on AWS or locally.

Common Libraries and Frameworks:

1. Express.js: Express.js is a minimalist web framework for Node.js, making it easy to build APIs and web applications. It provides robust routing, middleware support, and a simple, intuitive API.

```javascript
const express = require('express');
const app = express();

app.get('/api/resource', (req, res) => {
   // Retrieve data from DynamoDB or PostgreSQL
   res.json({ message: 'Data retrieved successfully' });
});

app.listen(3000, () => {
   console.log('Server is running on port 3000');
});
```

2. AWS SDK for JavaScript: The AWS SDK simplifies interaction with DynamoDB, allowing you to perform CRUD operations, manage tables, and handle authentication seamlessly.

```javascript
const AWS = require('aws-sdk');
AWS.config.update({ region: 'us-east-1' });
```

```
const docClient = new AWS.DynamoDB.DocumentClient();

// Example: Query DynamoDB
const params = {
  TableName: 'Table',
  Key: { id: '123' }
};

docClient.get(params, (err, data) => {
  if (err) console.error('Error:', err);
  else console.log('Data:', data);
});
```

3. **pg-promise:** pg-promise is a PostgreSQL library that provides a high-level interface for working with PostgreSQL databases, offering features like query building, parameterized queries, and transaction support.

```javascript
const pgp = require('pg-promise')();
const db = pgp('postgres://username:password@localhost:5432/database');

// Example: Query PostgreSQL
```

```
  db.one('SELECT * FROM users WHERE id = $1',
[userId])
    .then(data => {
      console.log('Data:', data);
    })
    .catch(error => {
      console.error('Error:', error);
    });
```

4. Express.js Middleware: Middleware functions in Express.js enable you to perform preprocessing tasks, such as authentication, request parsing, and error handling.

```javascript
// Middleware for logging requests
app.use((req, res, next) => {
  console.log(`${req.method} ${req.url}`);
  next();
});

// Middleware for error handling
app.use((err, req, res, next) => {
  console.error(err.stack);
  res.status(500).send('Internal Server Error');
});
```

Building RESTful Endpoints:

1. GET Endpoint: Retrieve data from DynamoDB or PostgreSQL.

```javascript
app.get('/api/resource/:id', (req, res) => {
    const resourceId = req.params.id;
    // Query DynamoDB or PostgreSQL based on resourceId
});
```

2. POST Endpoint: Create a new resource in DynamoDB or PostgreSQL.

```javascript
app.post('/api/resource', (req, res) => {
    const newData = req.body;
    // Insert newData into DynamoDB or PostgreSQL
});
```

3. PUT Endpoint: Update an existing resource in DynamoDB or PostgreSQL.

```javascript
```

```javascript
app.put('/api/resource/:id', (req, res) => {
    const resourceId = req.params.id;
    const updatedData = req.body;
    // Update resource with resourceId in DynamoDB or PostgreSQL
});
```

4. DELETE Endpoint: Delete a resource from DynamoDB or PostgreSQL.

```javascript
app.delete('/api/resource/:id', (req, res) => {
    const resourceId = req.params.id;
    // Delete resource with resourceId from DynamoDB or PostgreSQL
});
```

Authentication and Authorization:

Implement authentication and authorization mechanisms to secure your API endpoints. You can use JWT (JSON Web Tokens) for authentication and middleware for authorization checks.

Testing and Debugging:

Utilize tools like Postman for API testing and debugging. Write unit tests using libraries like Jest for server-side logic and ensure comprehensive test coverage.

By leveraging Express.js, AWS SDK for JavaScript, pg-promise, and middleware functions, you can build robust RESTful APIs with DynamoDB and PostgreSQL. Remember to focus on scalability, security, and performance optimization throughout the development process.

www.ingramcontent.com/pod-product-compliance
Lightning Source LLC
Chambersburg PA
CBHW031602210526
45464CB00004B/1396